AF235185

50 GAELIC COFFEE BREAKS

SHORT ACTIVITIES TO IMPROVE YOUR
SCOTTISH GAELIC ONE CUP AT A TIME

COFFEE BREAK LANGUAGES

Activities developed by

BOYD ROBERTSON

Introduction by

MARK PENTLETON

Series Editor

AVA DINWOODIE

CoffeeBreak
Gaelic

First published by Teach Yourself in 2026
An imprint of John Murray Press

I

Copyright © Coffee Break Languages 2026

The right of Coffee Break Languages to be identified as the Author of
the Work has been asserted by them in accordance with the Copyright,
Designs and Patents Act 1988.

All images © Shutterstock

All rights reserved. No part of this publication may be reproduced,
stored in a retrieval system, or transmitted, in any form or by any means
without the prior written permission of the publisher, nor be otherwise
circulated in any form of binding or cover other than that in which it
is published and without a similar condition being imposed on the
subsequent purchaser.

A CIP catalogue record for this title is available from the British Library

Paperback ISBN 9781399822589
ebook ISBN 9781399823302

Typeset by KnowledgeWorks Global Ltd.

Printed and bound in Great Britain by Clays Ltd, Elcograf S.p.A.

John Murray Press policy is to use papers that are natural, renewable
and recyclable products and made from wood grown in sustainable
forests. The logging and manufacturing processes are expected to
conform to the environmental regulations of the country of origin.

John Murray Press
Carmelite House
50 Victoria Embankment
London EC4Y 0DZ

Teach Yourself
Hachette Book Group
123 South Broad Street
Ste 2750
Philadelphia, PA 19109, USA

www.teachyourself.com

John Murray Press, part of Hodder & Stoughton Limited
An Hachette UK company

The authorised representative in the EEA is Hachette Ireland,
8 Castlecourt Centre, Dublin 15, D15 XTP3, Ireland (email: info@hbgi.ie)

CONTENTS

DÈ MU DHEIDHINN COFAIDH?

Hello! **Dè mu dheidhinn cofaidh?** Fancy a coffee? This book is designed to make it easy for you to learn just a little bit of Scottish Gaelic every single time you take a Coffee Break.

It is divided into three sections so that you can decide how long you've got and choose an activity that will fill whatever time you have. Is it just a quick espresso? A little longer for an americano or a latte? Whether you have 5, 10 or 15 minutes for your Coffee Break today, we have something to accompany your refreshment.

Throughout the book you will find a variety of activities, including reading texts, grammar exercises, writing tasks, idiom explanations and vocabulary practice.

Simply decide how long you have, choose an activity from the 5-, 10- or 15-minute Coffee Break section and start learning. **Nach tòisich sinn!**

ABOUT COFFEE BREAK LANGUAGES

Coffee Break Languages came into being in 2006 with the launch of the Coffee Break Spanish podcast. As the first podcast for beginners in Spanish, the idea of "learning a language on your coffee break" quickly took off, and soon learners around the world were using the Coffee Break Languages podcasts and online courses to build their language skills.

Since then the Coffee Break method has grown to cover 10 languages and has been recognised through numerous awards, including European Professional Podcast of the Year and the European Award for Languages.

The Coffee Break Languages team of language experts, teachers and native speakers is led by Mark Pentleton. A former high school languages teacher himself, Mark continues to share his passion for language learning, and the opportunities it provides, with learners around the world through podcasts, videos, courses and books.

INTRODUCTION
THE IMPORTANCE OF PRACTICE

MARK PENTLETON

"You've got to learn your instrument. Then you practise, practise, practise."

It was the virtuoso jazz saxophonist Charlie Parker who outlined the importance of practice in this way. Indeed, in a 1954 interview with fellow musician Paul Desmond, he explained that over the course of three or four years, he would spend up to 15 hours a day practising. This allowed him to master the improvisation skills which then led to the development of Bebop and influenced countless musicians who came after him.

No matter what skill you are acquiring, regular practice plays a crucial part. And don't worry, we're not suggesting 15 hours a day! You may well bake several hundred croissants before becoming confident in your ability to master the recipe. If you're doing the Couch to 5K running plan, you need to train regularly before you're ready to tackle those 5,000 metres.

And if your child happens to be learning to play the violin, then the old adage of "practice makes perfect" is probably something you say on a daily basis.

Your "instrument" is the Gaelic language. You can already play some notes on the instrument, and perhaps you can even manage a few tunes. You're probably at the stage now of wanting to "perform" these tunes, using the Gaelic you know in spoken and written situations, and perhaps even move on to more complex pieces. But before you reach this stage, there's something you must do. You've guessed it: practise!

As I said, there's no need to follow the same intense practice schedule of Charlie Parker, spending many hours a day on your language skills. Indeed, since our very first Coffee Break Languages lesson back in 2006, we've stressed the importance of "little and often" when it comes to improving your language skills. And that's exactly what this book is about.

We've brought together a collection of interesting and enjoyable exercises which will help you build your vocabulary, increase your understanding of grammar and develop a cultural awareness, all within the space of a "coffee break".

Through the exercises, you'll learn new words, see examples of grammar points that you know and learn new constructions. You'll complete reading challenges, acquire new idiomatic expressions and learn to describe what you see in a photo, a skill you can take into your daily life and practise your language wherever and whenever you want.

If you're training for a marathon, there's no doubt that the practice you put in beforehand is hard work. But language learning is not a marathon: it's a stroll in the park, a walk along a beach at sunset, or a drive along a beautiful lakeside as the early-morning mist clears. By ensuring that your practice is enjoyable, you'll make faster progress and you'll benefit from deeper learning. And that's exactly why we've written this book of fun and engaging exercises.

I started the introduction to this book with a quotation by Charlie Parker. However, I didn't give the full quotation. Having established the fact that, after learning the basics, what you need to do to master an instrument is "practise, practise, practise", Charlie Parker went on to add a third stage in this process:

"And then, when you finally get up there on the bandstand, forget all that and just wail."

That, in a sense, is what we're all aiming for as language learners. Of course, "wailing" may sound unpleasant and conjure up images of tears and despair, but in the context of jazz music, Parker was suggesting that if you've learned the tune and practised over and over again, then you are ready to fly, enjoying the moment and letting the music flow naturally. Having completed all the exercises in this book, I hope that you feel ready to "fly", "wail" or simply enjoy the moment, letting your language flow naturally using the new words, phrases and grammar points you've practised.

So, all you need to do now is decide how long you'd like to spend on your Gaelic today, pick any of our coffee break-length exercises, and begin your practice. I wish you "happy language learning" and, of course, "happy coffee breaking"!

HOW TO USE THIS BOOK

The activities in this book vary slightly in their difficulty from one to the next, but are generally around lower intermediate level, or A2–B1 on the CEFR. Remember that even if you find a particular activity a little easier, consolidation is a vital part of language learning and no learning is ever wasted.

ABBREVIATIONS

Before we get started, it may also help to familiarise yourself with a few abbreviations and features that you'll find throughout the book:

(m) - masculine noun

(f) - feminine noun

(f/m) - a noun that can be either feminine or masculine, depending on the dialect of Gaelic, but which is most commonly considered feminine

(m/f) - a noun that can be either feminine or masculine, depending on the dialect of Gaelic, but which is most commonly considered masculine

(m, pl) - masculine plural noun

(f, pl) - feminine plural noun

WRITING SPACE

✎____ This pencil followed by a line indicates a space for you to write your answers, but feel free to add your own notes in any blank spaces on the pages too.

CHECKLISTS

At the start of every section of the book you have a checklist, where you can record your Coffee Breaks by ticking off activities as you complete them.

ANSWERS SECTIONS

At the end of each activity, we'll tell you which page to turn to if there is an answers section. Take your time to read the examples and explanations that we give you. If there are words or phrases that are new for you, remember to use your dictionary to help you. You can use any space on the page or your own notebook to write this new vocabulary and help you remember it. There are also some extra pages at the back of this book where you can write your own notes.

TYPES OF ACTIVITY

Each of the three sections of this book contains a number of different types of activity. Below, you'll find a description of each type so that you know what to expect every time you choose an activity. Whether you're looking for some reading practice, a writing task, some help with grammar, or something else, we hope that these descriptions help you to decide how you're going to spend each Coffee Break.

5-MINUTE COFFEE BREAKS

Word Builder

In these activities, you will learn some interesting pieces of vocabulary on a variety of topics. There is then a short exercise to allow you to practise this vocabulary in context. To make the most of the Word Builder activities, we recommend writing down the words that are new to you in your own notes to help you remember them.

Mini Grammar Challenge

These challenges are designed to give you a little extra practice of some tricky Gaelic grammar points. Each activity will focus on one specific point and will include a brief explanation, an exercise and answers.

Idiomatically Speaking

In each of these activities, we will focus on one Gaelic idiomatic expression. First, we will explain its meaning and provide examples of some of the contexts in which the idiom can be used. Then there will be a short exercise or space for you to practise using the idiom in your own sentences.

Say What You See

In these writing activities, we will provide some suggested phrases to help you write a description of an image. As there is no set answer for this type of exercise, you may not know whether or not what you've written is entirely correct. Don't worry about this too much, however, as the purpose of these writing activities is simply to get you writing freely in Gaelic, practising creating different types of texts and, in this way, developing your writing skills. For these activities, we have included our own "answer", which we hope you will find useful to see. However, it's important to remember that there is no single correct answer, so don't worry if your description is very different.

Guided Translation

Each of these activities is based on a short piece of text in Gaelic: a well-known saying or a proverb. We will talk you through the language used in the piece of text to examine in detail the vocabulary and structures used and to help you come up with a good translation of it.

10-MINUTE COFFEE BREAKS

Translation Challenge

In these activities, your challenge is to translate sentences from English into Gaelic. There will be hints to help you, if you need them, and suggested translations and language explanations in the answers section.

Cultural Connections

These are designed to help you develop both your reading skills and your cultural knowledge. They are based on texts about a particular organisation associated with Gaelic culture and language, and include a vocabulary list and questions to help you test your understanding of the text.

Jumbled Letters

In these activities, you will be given a definition of a word in Gaelic and an anagram. Your task is to unscramble the letters of the anagram to find the word being defined. Then, test your knowledge of the language by seeing how many other Gaelic words you can make using those letters.

Number Focus

It takes a while, when learning a language, to reach the stage where you can instantly visualise the corresponding digit when you hear a number being said out loud. This can only become easier with practice, which is why our Number Focus activities include a variety of exercises, all designed to help you practise your numbers in Gaelic.

Taste Bud Tantaliser

These activities use recipes as reading texts and include a vocabulary list and a reading comprehension or language exercise so that you can practise your language skills while learning about a dish from Scotland. While the activity should only take around 10 minutes, there's nothing stopping you from getting to know the language in the recipe even better by following it and making the dish yourself when you have more time!

15-MINUTE COFFEE BREAKS

Reading Focus

These longer reading activities will allow you to study a short text about a particular aspect of culture in the Gaelic-speaking world. They include a vocabulary list, comprehension questions and language questions.

Grammar Focus

While the 5-minute Mini Grammar Challenges are perfect for a short bit of practice of specific grammar points, in these Grammar Focus activities we take a more in-depth look at different topics in Gaelic grammar, providing a more detailed explanation and a number of different exercises to help you practise.

Vocabulary Consolidation

This is a vocabulary drill exercise that will help you to familiarise yourself with pieces of vocabulary on a specific topic. Each activity focuses on 20 pieces of vocabulary and includes a number of different exercises to help you practise and get to know them.

5-MINUTE COFFEE BREAKS

CHECKLIST
5-MINUTE COFFEE BREAKS

Word Builder

Mini Grammar Challenge

Idiomatically Speaking

Say What You See

Guided Translation

1

AN T-SÌDE
WORD BUILDER

The weather can be quite changeable in Scotland and, of course, it is common to start a Gaelic conversation with a comment about the weather. In this activity, we're going to focus on some of the different words you can use to describe the weather in Gaelic. Have a look at the list below, then complete the exercise that follows to practise using these phrases. **Siuthad a-nis!**

* * *

tha i tioram - it is dry
tha i fliuch - it is wet
tha i fuar - it is cold
tha i blàth - it is warm
tha i teth - it is hot
tha i grianach - it is sunny
tha i brèagha - it is beautiful
tha i garbh - it is wild
tha i sgòthach - it is cloudy

tha i ceòthach - it is misty
tha an t-uisge ann - it is raining
tha reothadh ann - it is freezing
tha an sneachda ann - it is snowing
tha dealanaich is tàirneanaich ann - there is lightning and thunder

Here are some example sentences using this vocabulary:

> **Tha i uabhasach fuar an-diugh.**
> *It is very cold today.*

> **Tha i brèagha agus grianach ann an Dùn Èideann.**
> *It is beautiful and sunny in Edinburgh.*

> **Tha i sgòthach an seo ach chan eil an t-uisge ann.**
> *It is cloudy here but it isn't raining.*

> **Tha reothadh ann agus tha sneachda air na beanntan.**
> *It is freezing and there is snow on the hills.*

Note that Gaelic speakers in Skye generally use **tha e** instead of **tha i** in weather phrases.

Now you can practise using some of this new vocabulary by writing your own sentences on the lines below. Pick three locations around the world that you have visited or would like to visit and write a sentence for each, describing in Gaelic what you think the weather is like there today.

_____

_____

_____

_____

_____

_____

_____

_____

_____

_____

_____

_____

_____

_____

_____

2

BUADHAIREAN

MINI GRAMMAR CHALLENGE

In this Mini Grammar Challenge, we're going to practise using adjectives in Gaelic. Read the explanation below, then have a go at the short exercises that follow.

* * *

In Gaelic, the adjective normally comes after the noun it is describing and it takes different forms depending on whether the noun is masculine or feminine, singular or plural.

If the noun is masculine and singular, the adjective following it does not change from its base form (this is the form that you'd find in a dictionary). For example:

taigh beag
a small house (also the Gaelic for "a toilet"! In that case, it is written **taigh-beag.**)

latha math
a good day (also the greeting "good day")

falt bàn
fair hair, blond hair

If the noun is feminine, the adjective following it is lenited. This change in pronunciation is shown in writing by inserting an **h** as the second letter. For example:

beinn mhòr
a big mountain

oidhche mhath
a good night (also the expression "good night")

seacaid bhrèagha
a beautiful jacket

Some adjectives do not show lenition in writing. These are ones beginning with a vowel, or with **l, n, r, sg, sm, sp** or **st**. For example:

caileag òg
a young girl

litir laghach
a nice letter

EXERCISE I - COMBINE NOUN AND ADJECTIVE

Give the correct form of the adjective with the following nouns. The gender of the noun is shown with (m) for masculine and (f) for feminine.

1. **duine** (m) *a man* and **laghach** *nice*

   ✎_____

2. **lèine** (f) *a shirt* and **geal** *white*

   ✎_____

3. **fìon** (m) *wine* and **dearg** *red*

   ✎_____

4. **briogais** (f) *trousers* and **goirid** *short*

   ✎_____

5. **obair** (f) *work* and **ùr** *new*

   ✎_____

EXERCISE 2 - FILL IN THE GAPS

Complete the following sentences with the correct form of the adjective given in brackets.

1. **Tha taigh** (m) ✎_____ **aca.** (mòr)
   TRANSLATION: *They have a big house.*

2. **Tha dreuchd** (f) ✎_____ **aig Ceit.** (math)
   TRANSLATION: *Kate has a good job / post.*

3. **Tha càr** (m) ✎_____ **aig Seòras.** (geal)
   TRANSLATION: *George has a white car.*

4. **Tha sgiorta** (f) ✎_____ **air Anna. (uaine)**

TRANSLATION: *Anna is wearing a green skirt.*

5. **Tha lèine** (f) ✎_____ **agus taidh** (f)
✎_____ **air. (gorm, dubh)**

TRANSLATION: *He is wearing a blue shirt and a black tie.*

* * *

'S math a rinn thu! When you're happy with your answers, turn to page 71 to check them.

3

MÒR AIG A CHÈILE
IDIOMATICALLY SPEAKING

It's always interesting to learn idiomatic expressions in the language you're studying, especially when there isn't a direct equivalent in English. In this activity, we're going to focus on the Gaelic idiom **mòr aig a chèile**. This literally means "big at each other" and is used to convey that two people are very friendly with each other or are good friends.

Let's look at some examples to see this expression in context:

Tha Ceitidh agus Caitlin mòr aig a chèile.
Katie and Caitlin are pals.

Bha iad anns an sgoil còmhla agus tha iad mòr aig a chèile.
They were in school together and they are close friends.

Bha a' chlann mòr aig a chèile.
The children were very friendly with each other.

Chan eil an dà theaghlach mòr aig a chèile.

The two families are not on the best of terms.

Thusa nis! Can you come up with a few of your own examples? Use the lines below to write three of your own sentences using the expression **mòr aig a chèile.**

_____

_____

_____

_____

_____

_____

_____

_____

_____

_____

_____

_____

4

ANNS A' CHAFAIDH
SAY WHAT YOU SEE

What is happening in the picture below? In this activity you will practise your writing skills. On the next page is a list of suggested words and sentence starters to help you describe the scene. Use these to write three to five sentences about what you can see in the picture. **Siuthad!**

Anns a' chafaidh

SUGGESTED PHRASES

anns an dealbh tha - in the picture there is / there are
aig a' chùl - at the back
aig an aghaidh - at the front, in the foreground
air an làimh dheis / cheairt - on the right-hand side
air an làimh chlì - on the left-hand side
anns a' mheadhan - in the centre
cafaidh (f/m) - café
tha na caraidean ... - the friends are ...
a' suidhe / nan suidhe - sitting
na boireannaich (m, pl) - the women
an duine (m) - the man
a' gàireachdainn - laughing
ag òl - drinking
a' còmhdach aghaidh - covering his face
cofaidh (m) - coffee
tì (f) - tea
cupannan (m, pl) - cups
bòrd (m) - a table
lus (m) **beag** - a small plant
craobh (f) - a tree
bùird (m, pl) **sanasachd** - billboards
ad (f) - a hat
speuclairean (m, pl) - glasses
feusag (f) - a beard
mullach (m) **striopach** - striped top
sùilean (f, pl) - eyes
làmh (f) - a hand
gualainn (f) - a shoulder

Anns a' chafaidh

_____

_____

_____

_____

* * *

Now, if you'd like to see what we came up with, turn to page 72.

AN LÀMH A BHEIR, 'S I A GHEIBH
GUIDED TRANSLATION

In this Guided Translation, we're going to take an in-depth look at the language used in the following Gaelic proverb: **an làmh a bheir, 's i a gheibh.**

* * *

LANGUAGE EXPLANATION

Let's take a look at the language used in the proverb, word by word.

An is one of the forms of the definite article, "the".

Làmh is a feminine noun and means "hand".

A is a relative particle referring back to **làmh** and can be translated as "which" or "that". It is used again in this proverb before **gheibh**.

Bheir is the future tense of the irregular verb **thoir** ("give"). **Bheir**, therefore, means "will give". It is worth noting that there are 10 verbs in Gaelic that are called irregular because they do not adhere to a normal pattern in forming tenses. Among these verbs are **faic** ("see") and **cluinn** ("hear").

'S is an abbreviated version of the verb "to be", **is**. There are two forms of the verb "to be" in Gaelic. You will have already come across the positive present tense of the other form, **tha**. The **is** form, known grammatically as the copula, tends to be used for making assertions or statements linked to a noun. An example of the **is** form that you'll have come across very early in your Gaelic learning is **is mise ...** to say what your name is. **'S** can mean "is", "am" or "are", depending on the subject to which it refers. In this example, it refers directly to the following word, **i**.

As with languages such as French, nouns in Gaelic are either feminine or masculine. There are, therefore, two forms of personal pronoun: **i** for "she" or "it" (referring to a feminine noun) and **e** for "he" or "it" (referring to a masculine noun). The pronoun **i** in this saying refers to **làmh**, which is a feminine noun.

Gheibh is the future tense of another of the irregular verbs, **faigh** ("get"), and means "will get".

So now, can you work out what this proverb means? Write your translation on the lines below.

✎ _____

_____

_____

_____

_____

* * *

Once you are ready, turn to page 72 for the translation.

6

OBRAICHEAN
WORD BUILDER

Do you know how to talk about jobs in Gaelic? In this Word Builder, we're focusing on some of the words you can use to describe different jobs in Gaelic. Read the list below, then complete the exercise that follows to consolidate the new words you've learned.

* * *

nurs (f) / **banaltram** (f) - a nurse
dotair (m) - a doctor
tidsear (m/f) / **neach-teagaisg** (m) - a teacher
neach-lagh (m) - a lawyer
neach-frithealaidh (m) - a waiter / waitress, a shop assistant
rùnaire (m) - a secretary
manaidsear (m) - a manager
saor (m) - a joiner
seòladair (m) - a sailor
dràibhear (m) **bus / làraidh / trèana** - a bus / lorry / train driver

You'll see that three of the occupations listed above contain the word **neach**, meaning "a person". **Neach-lagh,** for example, is literally "a person of law" and, in the example further on, **neach-ciùil** is "a person of music".

There are two ways of stating a person's occupation in Gaelic. In this activity, we'll focus on one of these ways.

To say what job you do, you can say:

> **'S e ... a th' annam.**

For example:

> **'S e còcaire a th' annam.**
> *I'm a cook / chef.*

To say what job he does, you say:

> **'S e ... a th' ann.**

For example:

> **'S e iasgair a th' ann.**
> *He's a fisherman.*

To say what job she does, you say:

> **'S e ... a th' innte.**

For example:

> **'S e neach-ciùil a th' innte.**
> *She's a musician.*

Now complete the exercise to practise using these words without referring back to the vocabulary list if you can. Fill in the gap in each sentence to match the English translation.

1. 'S e ✎_____ a th' annam.
   TRANSLATION: *I am a lawyer.*

2. 'S e ✎_____ a th' ann.
   TRANSLATION: *He is a sailor.*

3. 'S e ✎_____ a th' innte.
   TRANSLATION: *She is a teacher.*

4. 'S e ✎_____ a th' annam.
   TRANSLATION: *I am a lorry driver.*

5. 'S e ✎_____ a th' innte.
   TRANSLATION: *She is a manager.*

6. 'S e ✎_____ a th' ann.
   TRANSLATION: *He is a chef.*

When you're ready, you can find the answers to the exercise on page 72.

If you'd like more practice with this new vocabulary, use the lines below to write some of your own sentences.

✎_____

_____

_____

_____

_____

_____

_____

_____

_____

_____

_____

_____

_____

7

AN TRÀTH LÀTHAIREACH
MINI GRAMMAR CHALLENGE

Verbs in Gaelic (apart from the verb "to be") do not have a simple present tense. The present tense of these verbs is formed by combining the verb "to be" with the verbal noun of the verb being used. The verbal noun, which can act as either verb or noun, is marked in English by the "-ing" ending.

In this Mini Grammar Challenge, we're going to look at how some verbal nouns are formed from the root of the verb. Read the explanation below, then have a go at the short exercises that follow. **Gabh romhad!**

* * *

There are several ways of forming the verbal noun from the root and it depends on the verb.

For a large number of verbs, you add **-adh** or **-eadh** to the root. If the last vowel in the root is broad (**a, o** or **u**), **-adh** is added. If the last vowel in the root is slender (**i** or **e**), **-eadh** is added.

For example:

> **glan** *clean* becomes **glanadh** *cleaning*
>
> **las** *light* becomes **lasadh** *lighting*
>
> **bris** *break* becomes **briseadh** *breaking*
>
> **till** *return* becomes **tilleadh** *returning*

For other verbs, you add **-ail** or **-eil** to the root. If the last vowel in the root is broad (**a**, **o** or **u**), **-ail** is added. If the last vowel in the root is slender (**i** or **e**), **-eil** is added. For example:

> **cùm** *keep* becomes **cumail** *keeping*
>
> **tog** *lift* becomes **togail** *lifting*
>
> **leig** *let / allow* becomes **leigeil** *letting / allowing*
>
> **tilg** *throw* becomes **tilgeil** *throwing*

Another way is to remove the last slender vowel (**i** or **e**) from the root and then add the **-adh** ending. For example:

> **dùin** *shut / close* becomes **dùnadh** *shutting / closing*
>
> **ullaich** *prepare* becomes **ullachadh** *preparing*

A further way is to add an **-e** to the root if the last vowel is slender (**i** or **e**). For example:

> **cluich** *play* becomes **cluiche*** *playing*
>
> **suidh** *sit* becomes **suidhe** *sitting*
>
> **ith** *eat* becomes **ithe** *eating*

*Note that the verbal noun "playing" can also be simply **cluich**.

Some verbal nouns do not change form at all from the root. For example:

fàs *grow* remains as **fàs** *growing*

ruith *run* remains as **ruith** *running*

òl *drink* remains as **òl** *drinking*

There is no easy way to know how the verbal noun is formed, but dictionaries usually provide the verbal noun form of each verb.

You should also know that verbal nouns beginning with a consonant are preceded by **a'** while those beginning with a vowel are preceded by **ag**. For example:

a' snàmh *swimming*

a' tòiseachadh *starting*

ag ionnsachadh *learning*

ag èisteachd *listening*

EXERCISE 1 - TRANSLATE

Translate the following Gaelic sentences into English.

1. **Tha iad a' fàs sgìth.**

  ✎ _____

  _____

2. **A bheil thu a' lasadh an teine?**

   ✎_____

   _____

3. **Chan eil Tormod a' cumail gu math.**

   ✎_____

   _____

4. **Cuin a tha an dannsa a' tòiseachadh?**

   ✎_____

   _____

EXERCISE 2 - FILL IN THE GAPS

Fill in the gaps in the sentences below with the correct form of the verbal noun.

1. **Cuin a tha sibh** ✎_____ ?
   TRANSLATION: *When are you returning?*

2. **Tha mi** ✎_____ **Gàidhlig.**
   TRANSLATION: *I'm learning Gaelic.*

3. **Bha Isla agus Lisa** ✎_____
   agus ✎_____ .
   TRANSLATION: *Isla and Lisa were eating and drinking.*

4. **Bha sinn** ✎_____ **agus**

   ✎_____ .

   TRANSLATION: *We were running and swimming.*

* * *

When you're happy with your answers, turn to page 73 to check them.

8

IS BEAG ORM
IDIOMATICALLY SPEAKING

In this activity, we're going to focus on another idiomatic expression in Gaelic, **is beag orm,** which means "I dislike" or "I really don't like". It is one of a number of idioms that start with the verb **is** followed by an adjective (here, **beag**), followed by a form of prepositional pronoun (here, **orm**). Another phrase with this structure that you'll already know well is **is toil leam** or **is caomh leam** ("I like"). **Is beag orm** literally means "it is little on me".

Let's see some examples of how this is used in context:

Is beag orm ceòl rap.
I dislike rap music.

Is beag orm a bhith ag èirigh tràth.
I dislike getting up early.

Is toil leam spòrs ach is beag orm criogaid.
I like sports but I really don't like cricket.

The **orm** part of the phrase can be replaced by **air** followed by a person's name.

For example:

Is beag air Karen matamataig.
Karen really doesn't like maths.

It can also be replaced by **air** on its own to refer to "he", or by **oirre** to refer to "she":

Is beag air an teas.
He doesn't like the heat.

Is beag oirre an t-uisge.
She dislikes the rain.

Thusa nis! Use the lines below to write three of your own sentences using the expression **is beag orm**.

_____

_____

_____

_____

_____

_____

_____

_____

_____

_____

31

9

ANNS A' PHÀIRCE
SAY WHAT YOU SEE

Take a close look at this photo and think about how you would describe what's happening in it. Use the suggested vocabulary and phrases on the next page to help you write a descriptive paragraph of three to five sentences about what you see in the photo.

SUGGESTED PHRASES

chì thu san dealbh ... - in the picture, you see ...

air an làimh dheis / cheairt - on the right

air an làimh chlì - on the left

aig an aghaidh - in the foreground

aig a' chùl - in the background

anns a' mheadhan - in the centre

pàirc(e) (f) - a park

ceum (m) / **frith-rathad** (m) - a path

craobhan (f, pl) - trees

feur (m) - grass

solais (m, pl) **sràide** - streetlights, streetlamps

sìde (f) **mhath** - nice weather

tòrr dhaoine - a lot of people

tha am boireannach ... - the woman is ...

tha am fireannach ... - the man is ...

eile - another

a' ruith - running

a' cluich spòrs - playing sport

a' falbh air baidhseagal - riding a bike

a' coiseachd - walking

air a' bhlàr a-muigh - outdoors

aodach (m) **spòrs** - sportswear

brògan (f, pl) **ruith** - running shoes

lèine (f) - a shirt

briogais (f) **ghoirid** - shorts

màthair (f) **agus nighean** (f) - a mother and daughter

leanabh (m) / **bèibidh** (m) - a baby

pram (m) - a pram, a stroller

Anns a' phàirce

_____

_____

_____

_____

* * *

Once you're happy with your paragraph, you can turn to page 73 to see an example answer.

10

THIG CRÌOCH AIR AN T-SAOGHAL
GUIDED TRANSLATION

This Guided Translation is based on a lovely saying in Gaelic. Read the language explanation, then write down your translation.

Thig crìoch air an
t-saoghal ach mairidh
gaol agus ceòl.

GAELIC PROVERB

Thig crìoch air an t-saoghal ach mairidh gaol agus ceòl.

GAELIC PROVERB

LANGUAGE EXPLANATION

Let's take a look at the language used in this saying, word by word.

Thig is the future tense form of the irregular verb **thig** and means "will come".

Crìoch is a noun meaning "end".

Air is the preposition "on".

An t- is a form of the definite article, "the".

Saoghal is a noun meaning "world" and is often used in the question **càit' air an t-saoghal?** ("where on earth?").

Next, we have **ach**, which is the conjunction "but" and is a word you'll see and hear often.

Mairidh is the future tense form of the regular verb **mair**, meaning "last" or "endure".

Gaol is a noun meaning "love" and you can use it in the expression **le gaol** at the end of a message or letter to say "with love".

Agus is the conjunction "and". Like **ach** above, you'll come across it frequently.

Ceòl is a noun meaning "music".

37

Can you work out now what this saying means? Write your translation on the lines below.

_____

_____

_____

_____

_____

* * *

Once you are ready, turn to page 74 for the translation.

11

CUR-SEACHADAN
WORD BUILDER

What do you like doing in your spare time? In this activity, we're going to practise using some words and phrases to talk about hobbies and pastimes. Read the vocabulary list below and then complete the exercise.

* * *

a' ruith - running
a' cluich goilf / ball-coise - playing golf / football
a' leughadh leabhar - reading a book
ag èisteachd ri ceòl - listening to music
a' còcaireachd - cooking
a' dol a-mach le caraidean - going out with friends
a' dol dhan taigh-dhealbh - going to the cinema
a' togail dhealbhan - taking photographs
ag obair sa ghàrradh - working in the garden

Here are some useful phrases and example sentences:

Dè 's toil leat a bhith a' dèanamh nuair a bhios tu saor?
What do you like doing in your free time? (literally "when you are free")

Nuair a bhios mi saor, is toil leam a bhith ...
In my free time, I like ...

Is toil leam a bhith a' dol a-mach le caraidean agus a' dol gu cuirmean-ciùil.
I like going out with friends and going to concerts.

Is toil le Ailios a bhith a' deasachadh biadh airson caraidean agus a' seinn ann an còisir.
Alice likes preparing food for friends and singing in a choir.

Note that Gaelic speakers in Lewis use **is caomh** instead of **is toil** for "like".

Now it's time to practise! Translate the following sentences into Gaelic.

1. In my free time, I like playing golf with friends.

   ✎ _____

   _____

   _____

2. Anna likes listening to music and running.

_____

_____

_____

3. James likes taking photographs and going to the cinema.

_____

_____

_____

Once you've had a go, turn to page 74 to check your answers.

For more practice, create some of your own sentences on the lines below, using this new vocabulary.

_____

_____

_____

_____

_____

_____

_____

_____

12

SEALBH

MINI GRAMMAR CHALLENGE

There are different ways of expressing possession in Gaelic. In this Mini Grammar Challenge, we're going to focus on one of these ways, which uses the preposition **aig** (meaning "at"). Read the explanation below, then complete the exercises that follow to test your knowledge. **Gabh romhad!**

* * *

USING AIG FOR POSSESSION

To say that someone has or possesses something, we start with the appropriate part of the verb "to be" followed by the item they own, then the preposition **aig** followed by the person's name. Let's start with some straightforward examples:

Tha càr aig Sìm.
Simon has a car. (literally "there is a car at Simon")

Tha peann aig Isla.
Isla has a pen.

Of course, we can add a description of the possession, too. For example:

Tha taigh snog aig Fiona 's Coinneach.
Fiona and Kenneth have a nice house.

We can ask about a possession using the question form of the verb "to be", **a bheil?**

A bheil cù aig Ciorstaidh?
Does Kirsty have a dog?

The answer to that would be either **tha** for "yes" or **chan eil** for "no".

If you want to say that someone doesn't have something, you'd say, for example:

Chan eil tiogaid aig Maya.
Maya doesn't have a ticket.

PREPOSITIONAL PRONOUNS

If we are not naming the person who has a particular possession, we combine the preposition **aig** with the relevant pronoun to give what are called prepositional pronouns. These are formed as follows:

aig + **mi** ("I / me")	=	**agam** ("my", literally "at me")
aig + **thu** ("you")	=	**agad** ("your", literally "at you")

aig + **e** ("he")	=	**aige** ("his", literally "at him")
aig + **i** ("she")	=	**aice** ("her", literally "at her")
aig + **sinn** ("we")	=	**againn** ("our", literally "at us")
aig + **sibh** ("you" formal / plural)	=	**agaibh** ("your", literally "at you")
aig + **iad** ("they")	=	**aca** ("their", literally "at them")

Now, let's see some examples of how these prepositional pronouns are used in context:

Chan eil iuchair agam.
I don't have a key.

A bheil airgead gu leòr agad?
Do you have enough money?

Tha fòn-làimhe ùr aice.
She has a new mobile phone.

A bheil cead-dràibhidh aige?
Does he have a driving licence?

Tha teaghlach aca.
They have a family.

IN THE PAST TENSE

You can change the tense of the verb "to be" in each sentence by changing **tha, chan eil** and **a bheil?** to **bha** ("was / were"), **cha robh** ("wasn't / weren't") and **an robh?** ("was? / were?").

Let's see some final examples:

Cha robh sgillinn agam.
I didn't have a penny.

An robh bata agad?
Did you have a stick?

Now it's over to you to put this into practice!

EXERCISE 1 - FILL IN THE GAPS

Complete the following sentences so that they match the English translations.

1. **Tha càr dearg** ✎_____ .
   TRANSLATION: *He has a red car.*

2. **Bha ùine gu leòr** ✎_____ .
   TRANSLATION: *We had plenty of time.*

3. **Bha leabhar** ✎_____ .
   TRANSLATION: *She had a book.*

4. **An robh teanta** ✎_____ ?
   TRANSLATION: *Did they have a tent?*

5. ✎_____ **Beurla aig Pierre ach chan eil Gàidhlig** ✎_____ .
   TRANSLATION: *Pierre has English but he doesn't have Gaelic / Pierre speaks English but not Gaelic.*

EXERCISE 2 - TRANSLATE

Use everything you've learned in this activity to translate the following sentences into Gaelic.

1. Does she have a dog?

   ✎_____

   _____

2. I have a white shirt.

   ✎_____

   _____

3. They have a new car.

   ✎_____

   _____

4. Did you have a coat?

   ✎_____

   _____

5. He had a blue boat.

   ✎_____

   _____

* * *

When you've finished, turn to page 74 to check your answers to the exercises.

13

CHAN EIL GUTH RI RÀDH
IDIOMATICALLY SPEAKING

In this activity, we're going to focus on a useful idiomatic expression that you can use in everyday conversation in Gaelic: **chan eil guth ri ràdh**. This literally means "there is not a voice to be said" and is generally used in response to a question to say that you "can't complain" or that you're "not too bad".

Let's see this expression used in context in the following questions and answers:

Ciamar a tha thu an-diugh? Och, chan eil guth ri ràdh.
How are you today? Oh, not too bad.

A bheil thu a' faireachdainn ceart gu leòr a-nis? Chan eil guth ri ràdh.
Are you feeling better now? I can't complain.

A bheil thu sgìth às dèidh dràibheadh astar cho fada? Chan eil. Chan eil guth ri ràdh.
Are you tired after driving such a long way? No, I'm not too bad.

Ciamar a tha an gnìomhachas na làithean seo? Chan eil ro dhona. Chan eil guth ri ràdh.

How is business these days? Not too bad. No reason to complain.

Thusa nis! Use the lines below to write three of your own sentences using the expression **chan eil guth ri ràdh.**

_____

_____

_____

_____

_____

_____

_____

_____

_____

_____

_____

_____

_____

14

ANNS A' CHIDSIN
SAY WHAT YOU SEE

How would you describe what's happening in the photo below? On the next page, you'll find some suggested sentence starters, phrases and vocabulary which will help you to practise your writing skills by describing the scene below. Use the lines on the following page to write a short description of three to five sentences.

SUGGESTED PHRASES

chì thu san dealbh ... - in the picture, you see ...

air an làimh dheis / cheairt - on the right

air an làimh chlì - on the left

aig an aghaidh / a' chùl - in the foreground / background

anns a' mheadhan - in the centre

triùir dhaoine - three people

dithis bhoireannach - two women

tha aon bhoireannach - one woman is

tha am boireannach eile - the other woman is

tha am fireannach - the man is

tha iad a' coimhead - they look / seem

toilichte - happy

a' còcaireachd - cooking

a' deasachadh biadh - preparing food

a' gàireachdainn - laughing

a' cur mun cuairt - stirring

aparan (m) - an apron

lèine (f) **bhreac** - a checked shirt

glainne (f) **fìon dearg** - a glass of red wine

dà ghlainne - two glasses

pana (m) **fraighigidh** - a frying pan

àmhainn (f) - an oven

glasraich (f) - vegetables

measan (m, pl) - fruit

pìos (m) **càise** - a piece of cheese

searbhadair shoithichean (m) - dish towel

falt (m) **bàn / dorcha** - fair / dark hair

sgeilpichean (f, pl) - shelves

leabhraichean (m, pl) - books
uinneag (f) - a window

Anns a' chidsin

_____

_____

_____

_____

_____

_____

* * *

Good work! If you'd like to see an example answer, turn to page 75.

15

AM FEAR NACH COIMHEAD ROIMHE
GUIDED TRANSLATION

Proverbs and sayings can be a great test for your translation skills, as they often contain more complex or poetic language. In this Guided Translation, we're looking at the following Gaelic proverb: **am fear nach coimhead roimhe, coimheadaidh e às a dhèidh.**

* * *

LANGUAGE EXPLANATION

Let's take a look at the language used in this proverb, word by word.

Am is one of the forms of the definite article, "the". It is used before masculine nouns beginning with the letter **b, f, m** or **p**.

Fear is a masculine noun meaning "man". It can also be translated as "he" or "one" when referring to a male or a masculine noun.

Nach is a negative conjunction that links the noun **fear** to the following verb. It can be translated as "who ... not" or "that ... not".

Coimhead is the verb "look".

Roimhe is an example of a prepositional pronoun and it means "before him". It comes from the preposition **ro** ("before").

Having just seen **coimhead** in the first part of this proverb, we now have **coimheadaidh**. This is the future tense form of the verb **coimhead** and translates as "will look".

The pronoun **e** is "he" (or "it" when referring to a masculine noun).

Finally, we have **às dèidh**, which is a prepositional phrase meaning "after". When the possessive **a** (meaning "his") is inserted into the phrase, **dèidh** is lenited to **dhèidh** and the phrase means "after him".

So, can you work out what this proverb means? Write your answer on the lines below.

✎ _____

_____

_____

_____

* * *

Once you're ready, turn to page 75 for the translation.

16

COLTAS
WORD BUILDER

In this activity, you will learn some words and phrases to describe a person's appearance. Take a close look at the vocabulary list below, then have a go at the exercise. We recommend noting down any words or phrases that are new to you to help you better remember them.

* * *

àrd - tall
mòr - big
beag - small
caol - thin
reamhar - stout
falt (m) **fada / goirid** - long / short hair
falt dualach / dìreach - curly / straight hair
falt bàn / dorcha / dubh / donn - fair / dark / black / brown hair
sùilean (f, pl) **gòrma / donn(a) / uaine** - blue / brown / green eyes
feusag (f) **fhada / ghoirid** - a long / short beard
stais (f) - a moustache

briogais (f) **fhada / ghoirid** - long / short trousers
lèine-T (f) - a T-shirt
sgiorta (f) - a skirt
seacaid (f) - a jacket
còta (m) - a coat
brògan (f, pl) **dubha / donn(a)** - black / brown shoes

Some useful phrases are:

> **Cò ris a tha i coltach?**
> *What is she like?*

> **Dè an t-aodach a th' air?**
> *What is he wearing?*

> **Tha sgiorta dhubh oirre.**
> *She is wearing a black skirt.*

> **Tha lèine ghorm air.**
> *He is wearing a blue shirt.*

Now it's over to you! Fill in the gaps in the sentences below by translating the word or phrase in brackets into Gaelic. Then write down the English translation of the full sentence.

1. **Tha còta** ✎_____ (*brown*) **air Ahmed.**

   ✎_____

   _____

2. **Tha lèine-T** ✎_____ (*white*) **air Zara.**

   ✎_____

   _____

3. **A bheil** ✎_____ (*fair hair*) **air Ciorstaidh?**

✎_____

_____

4. **Chan eil** ✎_____ (*a jacket*) **air Donna idir.**

✎_____

_____

5. **Tha** ✎_____ (*a short beard*) **agus**

✎_____ (*a moustache*) **air Gavin.**

✎_____

_____

Once you've had a go, turn to page 76 to check your answers.

For more practice, you can use the space below to write some of your own sentences in Gaelic, describing someone's appearance.

✎_____

_____

_____

_____

_____

_____

_____

_____

17

GNÌOMHAN CRÌOCHNAICHTE
MINI GRAMMAR CHALLENGE

In this Mini Grammar Challenge, we're going to practise using a form of the perfect and pluperfect tense in Gaelic. Read the explanation below, then have a go at the short exercises that follow. **Feuch ort!**

* * *

A common way of saying that an action has been completed in Gaelic is to place the preposition **air** ("on") before a verbal noun. If you want some practice of verbal nouns first, you can turn to Activity 7, "**An tràth làthaireach**".

Note that the **a'** or **ag** which is normally part of the verbal noun is dropped. If, for example, you want to say that Shona has arrived, you say **tha Shona air tighinn**, which literally means "Shona is on arriving". Similarly, if you want to say that time has run out, you say **tha an ùine air ruith**, the literal translation of which is "time is on running out".

Let's look at some more examples:

Tha a' bhùth air dùnadh.
The shop has shut / closed.

A bheil am bus air falbh?
Has the bus left?

To say that something *had* happened (in the pluperfect tense), you use the past tense form of the verb "to be" at the start of the sentence. For example:

Bha Sarah air sgrìobhadh.
Sarah had written.

Cha robh iad air èirigh.
They hadn't got up.

EXERCISE 1 - MATCHING PAIRS

Draw a line to match the pairs of opposite completed actions.

1. air seasamh	A. air tighinn
2. air fàgail	B. air fosgladh
3. air faighneachd	C. air stad
4. air dùnadh	D. air suidhe
5. air tòiseachadh	E. air freagairt

EXERCISE 2 - FILL IN THE GAPS

Complete the following sentences using the verb in brackets to express a completed action.

1. A bheil Siobhan agus Joe ✎_____ a-nis? (pòs)

2. Tha mi ✎_____ gu math. (ullaich)

3. Chan eil sinn ✎_____ ris fhathast. (èist)

4. Bha iad ✎_____ dhachaigh. (till)

5. An robh sibh ✎_____ dhan bhaile? (coisich)

* * *

Once you're happy with your answers, turn to page 76 to check them.

18

NACH BUIDHE DHUT!
IDIOMATICALLY SPEAKING

In this activity, we're going to focus on another of the many idiomatic expressions in Gaelic, **nach buidhe dhut!**, which means "aren't you lucky!". **Buidhe** is best known as the colour "yellow", but it also has less well-known meanings including "agreeable", "grateful" and "fortunate". In this expression, it means "fortunate" and the literal translation would be "isn't it fortunate to you!". The expression can be used to refer to different persons by changing the form of the preposition **do** from **dhut** to **dha, dhi, dhuibh,** and so on.

Here are some examples of how it is used:

— **Fhuair mi tiogaidean airson a' chonsairt.**
— **Nach buidhe dhut!**
— *I got tickets for the concert.*
— *Aren't you lucky!*

— Tha sinn a' falbh air làithean-saora aig deireadh na seachdain.
— Nach buidhe dhuibh!
— *We're going away on holiday at the end of the week.*
— *Aren't you lucky!*

Tha i a' faighinn àrdachadh pàighidh an-ath-mhìos.
Nach buidhe dhi!
She's getting a pay rise next month. Isn't she lucky!

Tha Cailean a' dol chun a' ghèama Eòrpach ann an Glaschu. Nach buidhe dha!
Colin is going to the European match in Glasgow. Isn't he lucky!

Thusa nis! Use the lines below to write three of your own sentences using the expression **nach buidhe dhut / dha / dhi / dhuibh / dhaibh!**

_____

_____

_____

_____

_____

_____

_____

_____

_____

_____

_____

_____

_____

_____

19

ANNS AN RÙM-TEAGAISG

SAY WHAT YOU SEE

In this activity, we're focusing on writing skills. Take a close look at the image below, then use the suggested vocabulary and phrases on the next page to help you write three to five sentences giving a short description of the scene. **Gabh romhad!**

SUGGESTED PHRASES

anns an dealbh seo, chì sinn ... - in this photo, we (can) see ...

rùm-teagaisg (m) - a classroom

clas (m) - a class

tha an neach-teagaisg / tidsear ... - the teacher is ...

a' lorg freagairt bho ... - looking for an answer from ...

a' dèanamh fiamh a' ghàire - smiling

a' comharrachadh aon sgoilear - pointing at one pupil

a' freagairt - answering

tha na sgoilearan ... - the pupils are ...

a' cur an làmhan suas - raising their hands

àireamhan (f, pl) - numbers

leasan (m) **àireamhachd** - an arithmetic lesson

cuistean (m) **meudachaidh** - sums

cuistean iomadachaidh - multiplications

air a' bhòrd dhubh - on the blackboard

aig an aghaidh - at the front

aig a' chùl - at the back

leabhar (m) - a book

deasg (m) - a desk

lèine (f) **gheal** - a white shirt

briogais (f) - trousers

peitean (m) - a cardigan

falt (m) **dubh** - black hair

falt bàn - fair hair

Anns an rùm-teagaisg

_____

_____

_____

_____

* * *

Once you're happy with your paragraph, you can turn to page 77 if you'd like to see an example answer.

20

TAIGH GUN CHÙ
GUIDED TRANSLATION

In this Guided Translation, we're going to take an in-depth look at the language used in another interesting Gaelic saying.

Taigh gun chù, gun chat, gun leanabh beag, taigh gun ghean, gun ghàire.

GAELIC PROVERB

Taigh gun chù, gun chat, gun leanabh beag, taigh gun ghean, gun ghàire.

GAELIC PROVERB

LANGUAGE EXPLANATION

Let's take a look at the language used in this saying, word by word.

Taigh is a noun meaning "house". It is frequently used as the first element of place names and takes the form "Tay" or "Ty" in English – for example, in the village names Taynuilt ("house of / by the stream") and Tyndrum ("house of / on the ridge") in Scotland. You might also come across the earlier spelling of **Taigh**, which is **Tigh**.

Gun is a preposition meaning "without". It causes the following word to be lenited. Lenition is usually shown in writing by placing an **h** as the second letter of the word. **Gun** is used repeatedly in this saying.

Cù is a noun meaning "dog". It is lenited after **gun**.

The next noun we have is an easy one, as **cat** is spelled the same in both Gaelic and English. Of course, here it is also lenited after **gun**, giving us **chat**.

Leanabh is a noun meaning "child". Remember that words beginning with **l**, **n** or **r** do not show lenition in writing.

Here, **leanabh** is described using the very common adjective **beag**, which means "small" or "little".

69

Gean is a noun meaning "cheer" or "good humour". Of course, it is lenited after **gun**.

Finally, we have the noun **gàire**, which means "laugh" or "laughter" and is lenited here following **gun**.

So now, do you know what this saying means? Write your translation on the lines below.

_____

_____

_____

_____

_____

* * *

When you're ready, you can find our translation on page 77.

2. BUADHAIREAN
Mini Grammar Challenge

EXERCISE 1 - COMBINE NOUN AND ADJECTIVE

1. duine **laghach**
2. lèine **gheal**
3. fìon **dearg**
4. briogais **ghoirid**
5. obair **ùr**

EXERCISE 2 - FILL IN THE GAPS

1. Tha taigh **mòr** aca.
2. Tha dreuchd **mhath** aig Ceit.
3. Tha càr **geal** aig Seòras.
4. Tha sgiorta **uaine** air Anna.
5. Tha lèine **ghorm** agus taidh **dhubh** air.

4. ANNS A' CHAFAIDH
Say What You See

HERE'S WHAT WE CAME UP WITH:

Anns an dealbh seo, tha na caraidean a' suidhe aig bòrd ann an cafaidh. Tha aon duine agus dithis bhoireannach ann. Tha na boireannaich a' gàireachdainn agus tha an duine a' còmhdach aghaidh agus a shùilean. Tha speuclairean air a' bhoireannach air an làimh dheis anns an dealbh agus tha mullach striopach air a' bhoireannach anns a' mheadhan. Tha làmh a' bhoireannaich air an làimh dheis air gualainn a' bhoireannaich eile. Tha ad agus feusag air an duine. Tha cupannan air a' bhòrd. Tha iad ag òl tì no cofaidh. Aig a' chùl, tha craobh agus bùird sanasachd agus tha lus beag air a' bhòrd.

5. AN LÀMH A BHEIR, 'S I A GHEIBH
Guided Translation

TRANSLATION: "The hand that gives is the hand that receives".

6. OBRAICHEAN
Word Builder

1. 'S e **neach-lagh** a th' annam.
2. 'S e **seòladair** a th' ann.
3. 'S e **tidsear / neach-teagaisg** a th' innte.
4. 'S e **dràibhear làraidh** a th' annam.
5. 'S e **manaidsear** a th' innte.
6. 'S e **còcaire** a th' ann.

7. AN TRÀTH LÀTHAIREACH
Mini Grammar Challenge

EXERCISE 1 - TRANSLATE

1. They are getting tired.
2. Are you lighting the fire?
3. Norman isn't keeping well.
4. When is the dance starting? / When does the dance start?

EXERCISE 2 - FILL IN THE GAPS

1. Cuin a tha sibh **a' tilleadh**?
2. Tha mi **ag ionnsachadh** Gàidhlig.
3. Bha Isla agus Lisa **ag ithe** agus **ag òl.**
4. Bha sinn **a' ruith** agus **a' snàmh.**

9. ANNS A' PHÀIRCE
Say What You See

HERE'S WHAT WE CAME UP WITH:

Chì thu san dealbh seo pàirc(e) le craobhan agus tòrr dhaoine. Tha sìde mhath ann. Air an làimh chlì aig an aghaidh, tha boireannach is fireannach a' ruith air frith-rathad sa phàirc(e). Tha aodach spòrs agus brògan ruith air an dithis aca agus tha iad a' bruidhinn ri chèile. Tha solais sràide air a' cheum agus chì thu anns a' mheadhan fireannach eile agus boireannach eile a' falbh air baidhseagal. Tha briogais ghoirid agus mullach geal air a' bhoireannach air a' bhaidhseagal agus tha briogais ghoirid is lèine air an fhireannach. Aig an aghaidh air an làimh

73

cheairt, tha màthair agus nighean a' coimhead air leanabh ann am pram air an fheur. Aig a' chùl, tha daoine a' coiseachd, a' ruith agus a' cluich spòrs.

10. THIG CRÌOCH AIR AN T-SAOGHAL
Guided Translation

TRANSLATION: "The world will come to an end but love and music will endure".

11. CUR-SEACHADAN
Word Builder

1. Nuair a bhios mi saor, is toil / caomh leam a bhith a' cluich goilf le caraidean.
2. Is toil / caomh le Anna a bhith ag èisteachd ri ceòl agus a' ruith.
3. Is toil / caomh le Seumas a bhith a' togail dhealbhan agus a' dol dhan taigh-dhealbh.

12. SEALBH
Mini Grammar Challenge

EXERCISE 1 - FILL IN THE GAPS

1. Tha càr dearg **aige.**
2. Bha ùine gu leòr **againn.**
3. Bha leabhar **aice.**
4. An robh teanta **aca?**
5. **Tha** Beurla aig Pierre ach chan eil Gàidhlig **aige.**

EXERCISE 2 - TRANSLATE

1. A bheil cù aice?
2. Tha lèine gheal agam.
3. Tha càr ùr aca.
4. An robh còta agad / agaibh?
5. Bha bàta gorm aige.

14. ANNS A' CHIDSIN
Say What You See

HERE'S WHAT WE CAME UP WITH:

Chì thu san dealbh triùir dhaoine, dithis bhoireannach agus fireannach, a' deasachadh biadh agus a' gàireachdainn. Tha iad a' coimhead toilichte a' còcaireachd. Tha falt fada bàn agus lèine bhreac air a' bhoireannach air an làimh chlì agus tha falt dorcha agus aparan air a' bhoireannach anns a' mheadhan. Tha falt goirid agus lèine bhreac air an fhireannach. Tha pana fraighigidh aig an fhireannach agus tha am boireannach sa mheadhan a' cur mun cuairt glasraich sa phana. Tha dà ghlainne fìon dearg, measan agus pìos càise air a' bhòrd. Tha uinneag air an làimh cheairt agus tha sgeilpichean agus àmhainn aig a' chùl. Tha leabhraichean air na sgeilpichean agus tha searbhadair shoithichean air a' bhòrd.

15. AM FEAR NACH COIMHEAD ROIMHE
Guided Translation

TRANSLATION: "He who doesn't look ahead will look back".

16. COLTAS
Word Builder

1. Tha còta **donn** air Ahmed.
   TRANSLATION: *Ahmed is wearing a brown coat.*
2. Tha lèine-T **gheal** air Zara.
   TRANSLATION: *Zara is wearing a white T-shirt.*
3. A bheil **falt bàn** air Ciorstaidh?
   TRANSLATION: *Does Kirsty have fair hair?*
4. Chan eil **seacaid** air Donna idir.
   TRANSLATION: *Donna isn't wearing a jacket at all.*
5. Tha **feusag ghoirid** agus **stais** air Gavin.
   TRANSLATION: *Gavin has a short beard and a moustache.*

17. GNÌOMHAN CRÌOCHNAICHTE
Mini Grammar Challenge

EXERCISE 1 - MATCHING PAIRS

1. **air seasamh**	D. **air suidhe**
2. **air fàgail**	A. **air tighinn**
3. **air faighneachd**	E. **air freagairt**
4. **air dùnadh**	B. **air fosgladh**
5. **air tòiseachadh**	C. **air stad**

EXERCISE 2 - FILL IN THE GAPS

1. A bheil Siobhan agus Joe **air pòsadh** a-nis?
   TRANSLATION: *Have Siobhan and Joe got married yet?*
2. Tha mi **air ullachadh** gu math.
   TRANSLATION: *I have prepared well.*

3. Chan eil sinn **air èisteachd** ris fhathast.
   TRANSLATION: *We haven't listened to it yet.*
4. Bha iad **air tilleadh** dhachaigh.
   TRANSLATION: *They had returned home.*
5. An robh sibh **air coiseachd** dhan bhaile?
   TRANSLATION: *Had you walked into the town?*

19. ANNS AN RÙM-TEAGAISG
Say What You See

HERE'S WHAT WE CAME UP WITH:

Anns an dealbh seo, chì sinn rùm-teagaisg le clas agus neach-teagaisg. Tha lèine gheal, peitean agus briogais air an tidsear agus tha falt dubh oirre. Tha fiamh a' ghàire air an neach-teagaisg agus tha leabhar aice na làimh. Tha an tidsear a' lorg freagairt bhon chlas agus tha na sgoilearan a' cur an làmhan suas. Tha i a' comharrachadh aon sgoilear aig a' chùl airson freagairt. Tha bòrd-dubh air a' bhalla agus tha cuistean meudachaidh is cuistean iomadachaidh air a' bhòrd-dhubh. Tha an clas a' dèanamh leasan àireamhachd. Tha na sgoilearan a' suidhe aig deasgaichean. Tha falt bàn air an sgoilear aig cùl an rùm-teagaisg.

20. TAIGH GUN CHÙ
Guided Translation

TRANSLATION: "A house without a dog, a cat or a child is a house without cheer or laughter".

10-MINUTE COFFEE BREAKS

CHECKLIST
10-MINUTE COFFEE BREAKS

Translation Challenge

Cultural Connections

Jumbled Letters

Number Focus

Taste Bud Tantaliser

21

EADAR-THEANGACHADH 1
TRANSLATION CHALLENGE

In this activity, we've given you some sentences in English to translate into Gaelic. Try translating the five sentences on your own first. Then, if you need some help, turn to the next page to find some hints. **Siuthad a-nis!**

* * *

1. Are you fluent in Gaelic? Not yet but I'm learning.

_____

_____

_____

2. Oliver likes the city but he doesn't like college.

_____

_____

_____

3. Amanda is going to the cinema with her friend tonight.

4. She is a musician. She plays the fiddle in a band.

5. It's not snowing just now but it's very cold.

HINTS

If you need some help, you may find the following hints useful.

1. You can use either the familiar or the formal form of the word for "you" in Gaelic.

2. Remember there are two ways of saying "like" in Gaelic. The appropriate form of the definite article ("the" in English) is required before the word for "college".

3. The preposition "to" following the verbal noun "going" can be based on either **do** or **gu / chun**. The noun after

do is in the dative case while the noun after **gu / chun** is in the genitive case.

4. You use the assertive form of the verb "to be" (also known as the copula) to say what job someone has. The continuous or habitual present tense as in "plays" is formed with the verbal noun, i.e. "is playing".

5. There are different ways of saying "very" in Gaelic depending on the dialect you use. Remember that some of these cause lenition in the following adjective while others don't.

* * *

Once you're happy with your answers, turn to page 155 to find our suggested translations and explanations.

22

SABHAL MÒR OSTAIG
CULTURAL CONNECTIONS

In this reading text, you'll learn about an important centre of Gaelic culture and education, Sabhal Mòr Ostaig. Use the vocabulary list to help you as you read through it, then answer the questions on the following page to test your understanding. Read the text as many times as you need to. **Gabh romhad!**

* * *

Tha Sabhal Mòr Ostaig, an t-Ionad Nàiseanta airson Cànan is Cultar na Gàidhlig, suidhichte ann an ceann a deas an Eilein Sgitheanaich. Chaidh a stèidheachadh ann an 1973 ann an seann sabhal ann an Slèite le Sir Iain Noble, a bha air oighreachd mhòr a cheannach san sgìre. An toiseach, b' e cùrsaichean goirid airson luchd-ionnsachaidh a bha aig a' Cholaiste agus b' ann an 1983 a thòisich cùrsaichean làn-ùine. Tha Sabhal Mòr air fàs gu mòr tro na bliadhnaichean is tha e an-diugh na cholaiste àrd-fhoghlaim agus na phàirt de dh'Oilthigh na Gàidhealtachd is nan Eilean. Faodaidh oileanaich cùrsaichean ceuma suas gu ìre na dotaireachd a dhèanamh an dà chuid aig a' Cholaiste fhèin agus air astar. Tha cùrsaichean goirid air an tabhann fhathast is bidh na ceudan a' tighinn thuca gach samhradh bho air feadh an t-saoghail. Tha mòran oileanach eadar-nàiseanta cuideachd a' dèanamh nan cùrsaichean ceuma tro ionnsachadh air-loidhne. Tha làrach àlainn na Colaiste air leudachadh gu mòr agus tha an togalach as ùire air ainmeachadh às dèidh Iain Noble.

VOCABULARY

Ionad (m) **Nàiseanta** - National Centre
suidhichte - situated
stèidhich - establish
sabhal (m) - barn
oighreachd (f) - estate
ceannaich - buy, purchase
luchd-ionnsachaidh (m, pl) - learners
làn-ùine - full-time
colaiste (f) **àrd-fhoghlaim** - higher education college
Oilthigh na Gàidhealtachd is nan Eilean - University of the Highlands and Islands
faodaidh - may, can
oileanach (m) - student
cùrsa (m) **ceum** - degree course
ìre (f) **na dotaireachd** - doctorate level
air astar - at a distance, remotely
air an tabhann - offered
air feadh - throughout
saoghal (m) - world
eadar-nàiseanta - international

air-loidhne - online
làrach (f) - campus, site
air leudachadh - expanded
togalach (m) - building
air ainmeachadh - named

COMPREHENSION QUESTIONS

Answer the following questions in English.

1. What information are we given about Sir Iain Noble?

   _____

   _____

2. What did the college provide initially?

   _____

   _____

3. What happened in 1983?

   _____

   _____

4. What higher education courses are currently offered at the college?

   _____

   _____

5. What is said about the college campus and about a
   particular building?

   _____

   _____

* * *

When you're ready, turn to page 158 to check your answers.

23

ANAGRAM 1

JUMBLED LETTERS

In this activity, you'll find two definitions and two words whose letters have been jumbled up. Your task is to unscramble the letters to find the words being defined. If you need some help, turn to page 92 to find a hint. Then see how many other words in Gaelic (of three or more letters) you can make using the letters from the anagram. **Gur math a thèid leat.**

* * *

I. DEFINITION: **canar seo ri cuideigin à aon de dh'eileanan na h-Alba.**

CAHASÒLHED

✎ _____   _____

_____   _____

_____   _____

_____   _____
_____   _____
_____   _____
_____   _____
_____   _____
_____   _____
_____   _____
_____   _____

2. DEFINITION: **bidh an neach seo a' gabhail pàirt ann an geamannan.**

RACLDEHIIAUC

_____   _____
_____   _____
_____   _____
_____   _____
_____   _____
_____   _____
_____   _____
_____   _____
_____   _____
_____   _____

HINTS

1. This can be both a noun and an adjective.
2. This is a masculine noun which is linked to a verb.

* * *

When you're ready, turn to page 158 to check your answers.

24

DÒIGHEAN CUNNTAIS
NUMBER FOCUS

In this activity, we're going to practise counting in Gaelic. Read through the explanation given below if you need a reminder of how numbers work in Gaelic, then complete the exercises that follow.

* * *

There are two counting systems in use in Gaelic. One of these is based on 10s, the other on 20s. The numbers 1–20 are the same in both systems.

1–19

The numbers 1–10 are:

1. aon
2. dhà
3. trì
4. ceithir

5. còig	8. ochd
6. sia	9. naoi
7. seachd	10. deich

The numbers 11–19 build on these by adding **deug** (or **dheug**), which is equivalent to the element "teen" in English. So, 11 is literally "one teen" (**aon deug**), 12 is "two teen" (**dà dheug** – **dà** causes lenition in the next word), 13 is "three teen" (**trì deug**) and so on up to **naoi deug** ("nineteen").

20–29

"Twenty" is **fichead** in both systems and the pattern for numbers 21 to 29 is to add the number onto the 20, as in **fichead sa dhà** (22) and **fichead sa sia** (26). Where the number to be added begins with a vowel, it is preceded by **h-**, as in **fichead sa h-aon** (21) and **fichead sa h-ochd** (28).

30–59

The number 30 is **fichead sa deich** in the system based on 20s but becomes **trithead** in the system based on 10s. Numbers from 31 to 39 based on **fichead** repeat the same pattern as the numbers 21–29, giving you numbers such as **fichead sa seachd deug** for 37 and **fichead sa h-ochd deug** for 38. Numbers 31–39 based on 10s add the numbers 1–9 to **trithead**: for example, **trithead sa còig** (35).

The number 40 is either **dà fhichead** or **ceathrad**, depending on which system you are using, and the numbers up to 49 are based on these in the same way as 20–29.

The number 50 is **dà fhichead sa deich** using the 20 system or **caogad** using the 10 system. Both systems also use **leth-cheud**, which is literally "half a hundred" and is the most commonly used option.

60–100

The numbers 60 to 99 are based on the patterns set out above. The single-word forms for 60, 70, 80 and 90 in the 10 system are **seasgad**, **seachdad**, **ochdad** and **naochad**. The equivalents in the 20 system are **trì fichead**, **trì fichead sa deich**, **ceithir fichead** and **ceithir fichead sa deich**. "A hundred" is **ceud** in both systems.

Thusa nis! Use the information given above to complete the following exercises.

EXERCISE 1 - LOWEST TO HIGHEST

Place the numbers below in order from lowest to highest.

a) **seasgad sa dhà**
b) **fichead sa h-aon**
c) **seachdad sa h-ochd**
d) **ceithir fichead sa còig**
e) **ceathrad sa ceithir**

LOWEST   1. ✎_____

          2. ✎_____

          3. ✎_____

          4. ✎_____

HIGHEST   5. ✎_____

EXERCISE 2 - CONVERT

Convert the numbers below into the other system. We've done the first one for you.

> **trìthead sa sia** → *fichead sa sia deug*

1. **trì fichead sa trì**

   ✎_____

2. **naochad sa naoi**

   ✎_____

3. **dà fhichead sa seachd**

   ✎_____

4. **seasgad sa h-ochd**

   ✎_____

5. **ceithir fichead sa sia**

   ✎_____

* * *

Once you have finished, you can find the answers on page 160.

25

CLÀR-SIÙCAIR
TASTE BUD TANTALISER

Below is a recipe for **clàr-siùcair** ("tablet"), which is a popular sweet treat in Scotland. It's very easy to make with just a few simple ingredients – and once you try it you'll fall in love with it!

Read the list of ingredients and the instructions, then answer the comprehension questions that follow to test your understanding.

* * *

STUTHAN A DHÌTH

250 g ìm saillte no ìm neo-shaillte
900 g siùcar gràinneach
300 ml bainne
crogan 397 g bainne milis / co-dhlùthaichte
spàin tì faoineig

DEASACHADH

1. Suath rud beag ìme air tiona de mheud c 20 × 15 cm.
2. Lìnig an tiona le pàipear bèicidh.
3. Cuir na stuthan uile còmhla ann am pana.
4. Cuir gach rud mun cuairt aig teas ìosal gus an leagh an siùcar gu lèir.
5. An dèidh sin, thoir chun na goil' e is goil e gus an ruig e 120 C air teas-mheidh siùcair. Cuir am measgachadh mun cuairt fhad 's a tha e a' goil.
6. Nuair a ruigeas am measgachadh an teas ceart, thoir bhàrr an teas e.
7. Cuir an fhaoineag na cheann agus cuir mun cuairt e gu làidir airson faisg air còig mionaidean.
8. Fàsaidh am measgachadh nas tighe mar a tha e a' fuarachadh.
9. Dòirt an stuth dhan tiona leis an lìnigeadh agus leig leis seatlaigeadh. Dèan e cho rèidh is as urrainn dhut.
10. Nuair a dh'fhàsas am measgachadh nas fhuaire, geàrr e ann an ceàrnagan beaga le sgian gheur.

VOCABULARY

stuth a dhìth (m) - ingredient
ìm (m) **saillte** - salted butter
neo-shaillte - unsalted
siùcar (m) **gràinneach** - granulated sugar
crogan (m) - tin, can
bainne (m) **milis / co-dhlùthaichte** - condensed milk
spàin (f) **tì** - teaspoon

faoineag (f) - vanilla

deasachadh (m) - preparation

suath - rub

rud (m) - a thing, a bit

tiona (m) - baking tin

de mheud - size

lìnig, lìnigeadh - line, lining

pàipear (m) **bèicidh** - baking paper

cuir còmhla - put together, mix

cuir mun cuairt - stir

teas (m) - heat

ìosal - low

leagh - melt

gu lèir - altogether, completely

thoir - bring

chun na goile - to the boil

ruig - reach

teas-mheidh (f) **siùcair** - sugar thermometer

measgachadh (m) - mixture

fhad 's - while

nuair - when

bhàrr - from

cuir na cheann - add

gu làidir - strongly, vigorously

faisg air - near, nearly

fàsaidh - will grow

nas tighe - thicker

a' fuarachadh - cooling

dòirt - pour

stuth (m) - stuff, material
leig leis - allow it
seatlaig - settle
dèan - make
cho rèidh - as even
as urrainn dhut - as you can
nas fhuaire - cooler, colder
geàrr - cut
ceàrnag (f) - square
geur - sharp

EXERCISE 1 - REORDER

Put the following instructions into the correct order so that they match the directions given in the recipe.

a) Make it as smooth as you can.
b) Stir it vigorously.
c) Cut it into small squares.
d) Line the tin with baking paper.
e) Pour the material into the tin.
f) Mix all the ingredients.

ORDER OF STEPS: ✎_____

EXERCISE 2 - FIND THE GAELIC

Now find the Gaelic for the following phrases in the text. Note that they don't appear in the order given below.

1. let it settle

   ✎_____

2. take it off the heat

   ✎_____

3. add the vanilla

   ✎_____

4. melt all the sugar

   ✎_____

5. while it's boiling

   ✎_____

6. a little bit of butter

   ✎_____

* * *

Once you've finished the exercises, turn to page 160 to check your answers.

26

EADAR-THEANGACHADH 2
TRANSLATION CHALLENGE

Translate the following sentences into Gaelic. Have a go on your own first, then if you need some help, turn to the next page to find a hint for each sentence. **Siuthad a-nis!**

* * *

1. I think they are coming tomorrow morning.

2. Sarah is a designer. She works from home.

3. I saw a good programme about that on television last night.

✎_____

_____

_____

4. Have you ever been at a music festival in the islands?

✎_____

_____

_____

5. The plane lands on the beach in Barra.

✎_____

_____

_____

HINTS

If you need some help, you may find the following hints useful.

1. You need to use the linking form of the verb "to be" in the second half of sentence 1.
2. You need to use two different forms of the verb "to be" in these two short sentences.
3. Remember that the verb "to see" is irregular in form.

4. There are several words for "ever" in Gaelic, but there is only one that is used in a past tense context.

5. Nouns beginning with **p** or **b** require a different form of the definite article ("the" in English).

* * *

Once you're happy with your answers, turn to page 161 to find our suggested translations and explanations.

27

FÈISEAN
CULTURAL CONNECTIONS

This reading comprehension activity is based on a text about **fèisean** or "festivals". Use the vocabulary list to help you with any unfamiliar words as you read through it, then answer the comprehension questions that follow. If you'd like an extra challenge, try reading the text and answering the questions before looking at the vocabulary list. Remember, it's always there if you need some help.

* * *

Tha fèisean air fàs cumanta ann an Alba bhon a chaidh a' chiad fhèis a cumail ann am Barraigh ann an 1981. Aig an àm sin, bha pàrantan agus daoine eile san eilean a' gabhail dragh nach robh a' chlann ag ionnsachadh mu cheòl traidiseanta ann am foghlam foirmeil san sgoil. Gus sin a chur ceart, chuir iad romhpa fèis a chumail as t-samhradh nuair a bhiodh na sgoiltean air làithean-saora. Chaidh cho math leis a' chiad

Fhèis Bharraigh gun do bhrosnaich e pàrantan ann an eileanan eile fèisean coltach ris a chumail.

Tha na fèisean a' toirt cothrom do dh'òigridh ann an coimhearsnachd tighinn còmhla airson na sgilean aca sna h-ealain Ghàidhlig a leasachadh ann an suidheachadh neo-fhoirmeil. Bidh iad ag ionnsachadh ionnsramaidean ciùil, òrain thraidiseanta, dannsa Gàidhealach is dràma fad còig latha is bidh cèilidh air a chumail air an oidhche mu dheireadh. Tha cuid dhe na fèisean a' ruith prògram de chlasaichean fad na bliadhna airson sgilean an òigridh a leasachadh.

An-diugh tha dà fhichead sa seachd fèis air feadh Alba is tha mu shia mìle duine òg a' gabhail pàirt annta gach bliadhna.

VOCABULARY
cumanta - common
Alba (f) - Scotland
bhon - since
chaidh a chumail - has been held
Barraigh (m) - Barra
àm (m) - time
pàrant (m) - parent
daoine eile - other people
a' gabhail dragh - becoming concerned
clann (f) - children
foghlam (m) **foirmeil** - formal education
gus - in order to
chuir iad romhpa - they planned
as t-samhradh (m) - in summer

làithean-saora (m, pl) - holidays

brosnaich - encourage

coltach ris - similar

a' toirt cothrom - giving an opportunity

òigridh (f) - youth

coimhearsnachd (f) - community

còmhla - together

sgil (f/m) - skill

ealain (f) - art

a leasachadh - to develop

suidheachadh (m) - situation

neo-fhoirmeil - informal

ionnsramaid (f) **ciùil** - musical instrument

òran (m) - song

dannsa (m) - dance

fad (m) - duration

mu dheireadh - last

cuid - some

bliadhna (f) - year

air feadh - throughout

gabh pàirt - take part, participate

annta - in them

COMPREHENSION QUESTIONS

Answer the following questions in English.

1. What happened in 1981?

   ✎_____

   _____

2. What concern did parents and other islanders have?

   ✎_____

   _____

3. What solution did they propose?

   ✎_____

   _____

4. What is the duration of a **fèis** and how does it finish?

   ✎_____

   _____

5. What are we told about the growth of the **fèisean**?

   ✎_____

   _____

* * *

Once you're happy with your answers, you can turn to page 164 to check them.

28

ANAGRAM 2
JUMBLED LETTERS

In this anagram challenge, your task is to unscramble the letters of the two anagrams to find the words being described in the definitions. If you need some help, turn to page III to find a hint for each anagram. Then see how many other words in Gaelic (of three or more letters) you can make using the letters from the anagram.

* * *

I. DEFINITION: **bidh thu faighinn fios bho seo.**

A H D I C E N D A H

_____   _____
_____   _____
_____   _____
_____   _____
_____   _____
_____   _____

2. DEFINITION: 's dòcha gun can thu seo às dèidh biadh a ghabhail no rudeigin a dhèanamh.

CATIRAHIER

_____   _____
_____   _____
_____   _____
_____   _____
_____   _____
_____   _____
_____   _____
_____   _____
_____   _____
_____   _____

HINTS

1. This is a feminine noun and its plural form is often used too.

2. This is an adjective formed from part of a verb.

* * *

When you're ready, you can find the anagram solutions on page 164.

29

DÈ 'N UAIR A THA E?
NUMBER FOCUS

In this activity, we're going to practise numbers in the context of time. We'll start with a quick reminder about how to tell the time in Gaelic, then do some exercises to practise using numbers. **Siuthad a-nis!**

* * *

To ask what the time is in Gaelic, you say **dè 'n uair a tha e?** and to say what time it is, you say, for example, **tha e seachd uairean** ("it's seven o' clock", literally "it's seven hours"). "A half hour" is **leth-uair** and "half past" is **leth-uair an dèidh. Madainn** and **feasgar** are used to distinguish between am and pm.

EXERCISE I - WHEN?

Read the following statements and answer the questions in English.

1. **Tha na naidheachdan air an telebhisean aig sia uairean.**

   When is the news on television?

   ✎ _____

2. **Bidh an trèan dhan Òban a' falbh aig dà uair feasgar.**

   When does the train to Oban depart?

   ✎ _____

3. **Bidh consairt na Fèise a' tòiseachadh aig leth-uair an dèidh seachd.**

   When does the Fèis concert start?

   ✎ _____

4. **Ràinig iad Colaiste na Gàidhlig mu aon uair deug.**

   When did they reach the Gaelic College?

   ✎ _____

5. **Thòisich a' cho-labhairt aig naoi uairean sa mhadainn Diardaoin.**

   When did the conference begin?

   ✎ _____

EXERCISE 2 - ADD THE TIME

Complete the sentences below by writing the times given in brackets. Write out each time-phrase in full in Gaelic. For example:

2:30 pm
leth-uair an dèidh a dhà feasgar

1. **Bidh an t-aiseag a' ruighinn an eilein aig** ✎_____
_____. (5 pm)

2. **Chì mi thu aig an stèisean aig** ✎_____
_____. (10:30)

3. **Cha bhi mi a-staigh gu** ✎_____
_____. (8 pm)

4. **Tha prògram math air an rèidio a-nochd aig** ✎_____
_____. (9:30)

5. **Feumaidh sinn falbh aig** ✎_____
_____. (6:30 am)

* * *

The answers to these exercises can be found on page 165.

30

ARAN-MILIS
TASTE BUD TANTALISER

Aran-milis or "shortbread" is very popular in Scotland. It is usually an accompaniment to tea or coffee but also features as part of some desserts. It's easy to make with just a few simple ingredients. Use the vocabulary list provided to help you read through this recipe for **aran-milis,** then answer the questions that follow to test your understanding.

* * *

STUTHAN A DHÌTH

450 g flùr lom / plèan
220 g semolina no rus pronn
220 g siùcar castair
450 g ìm
25 g ìm leaghte airson an tiona bèicearachd a shuathadh

DEASACHADH

1. Bruisig an treidhe bèicearachd (26 × 22 cm) leis an ìm leaghte.
2. Criathraich am flùr, an semolina (no an rus pronn) is an siùcar castair do bhobhla measgachaidh.
3. Geàrr an t-ìm is cuir e an lùib na stuthan tioram.
4. An uair sin, suath a-steach e le do mheuran gus an tèid e na thaois.
5. Brùth an taois aran-milis gu cothromach thairis air an treidhe bhèicearachd gu lèir.
6. Cleachd forca gus sreathan rèidh de bhioran forca a dhèanamh thairis air an uachdar gu lèir.
7. Bruich e ann an àmhainn aig teas ìosal (150 C) airson mu uair gu leth.
8. Thoir an treidhe às an àmhainn nuair a bhios dath aotrom òrdha air agus dustaig e le crathadh de shiùcar castair.
9. Às dèidh mu dheich mionaidean, geàrr an t-aran-milis ann an ceàrnagan cothromach agus fàg e san treidhe gus am fàs e fuar.

VOCABULARY

flùr (m) **lom / plèan** - plain flour
rus (m) **pronn** - rice flour
siùcar (m) **castair** - caster sugar
ìm (m) **leaghte** - melted butter
bèicearachd (f) - baking
suath - rub
bruisig - brush

treidhe (f/m) - tray

criathraich - sieve

bobhla (m) - bowl

measgachadh - mixing

geàrr - cut

cur an lùib - mix, blend

suath a-steach - rub in

meuran (f/m, pl) - fingers

gus an tèid e - until it goes

taois (f) - dough

brùth - press

gu cothromach - evenly

thairis - across, over

gu lèir - completely, altogether

cleachd - use

gus - so that

sreath (f/m) - row

rèidh - even

bioran (m, pl) **forca** - fork pricks

a dhèanamh - to do / make

uachdar (m) - surface

bruich ann an àmhainn - bake in the oven

teas (m) - heat

ìosal - low

mu - about

uair gu leth - an hour and a half

thoir - take

dath (m) - colour

aotrom - light

òrdha - golden

dustaig - dust
crathadh (m) - sprinkle
às dèidh - after
ceàrnag (f) - square
cothromach - regular
fàg - leave
fàs - grow, get

EXERCISE 1 - COMPREHENSION

Answer the following questions in English.

1. For what purpose is the smallest quantity of ingredient used?

   ✎ _____

   _____

2. Where are the sieved ingredients put?

   ✎ _____

   _____

3. What are you told to do with a fork?

   ✎ _____

   _____

4. How long should the baking process take?

   ✎ _____

   _____

5. How long should you wait before cutting the shortbread into pieces?

_____

_____

EXERCISE 2 - FIND THE GAELIC

Now find the Gaelic for the following phrases in the text. Note that they don't appear in the order given below.

1. bake it in an oven

   _____

2. dust it with a sprinkle of caster sugar

   _____

3. sieve the flour

   _____

4. leave it in the tray until it cools

   _____

5. rub it in with your fingers

   _____

* * *

Well done! You'll find the answers to the exercises on page 166.

31

EADAR-THEANGACHADH 3
TRANSLATION CHALLENGE

In this Translation Challenge, you have some sentences in English to translate into Gaelic. If you need some help, you can find a hint for each sentence on the following page. **Gabh romhad!**

* * *

1. Which one do you want? The old one or the new one?

   ✎ _____

   _____

   _____

2. She likes gin but he prefers whisky.

   ✎ _____

   _____

   _____

3. Have you met them yet? No.

  ✎_____

  _____

  _____

4. We hope to do that sometime next year.

  ✎_____

  _____

  _____

5. Where do you want to go after dinner?

  ✎_____

  _____

  _____

HINTS

If you need some help, you may find the following hints useful.

1. "One" can be either masculine or feminine.
2. There are two ways of expressing "like" in Gaelic.
3. Past tense questions usually begin with **an do?**
4. To express hope, you use the continuous present form of the verb.
5. "Want" can be translated in two different ways.

* * *

Once you're happy with your translations, turn to page 167 to find our suggested translations and explanations.

32

AM MÒD NÀISEANTA RÌOGHAIL

CULTURAL CONNECTIONS

The text below is all about **Am Mòd Nàiseanta Rìoghail,** the Royal National Mòd. Read the text, use the vocabulary list on the next page to help you with any unfamiliar words, then answer the comprehension questions that follow to test your understanding. **Feuch ort!**

* * *

Tha Am Mòd Nàiseanta Rìoghail air a chumail anns an Dàmhair gach bliadhna. 'S e Am Mòd Nàiseanta an fhèis as motha ann an saoghal na Gàidhlig agus 's e an cruinneachadh as motha de luchd-labhairt na Gàidhlig anns a' bhliadhna. Chaidh a' chiad Mhòd Nàiseanta a chumail san Òban còrr is ceud bliadhna air ais ach tha am Mòd a-nis air a chumail ann an diofar àite gach bliadhna. Bidh am Mòd a' tòiseachadh air Dihaoine le fosgladh oifigeil is cuirm-chiùil mhòr agus a' tighinn gu ceann seachdain Disathairne le cruinneachadh de na còisirean mòra. Tha mòran fharpaisean aig a' Mhòd – farpaisean seinn, ciùil, aithris bàrdachd is sgeulachd, dràma, litreachais agus iomain. 'S iad na farpaisean airson nam Bonn Òr ann an seinn aon-neach na farpaisean as ainmeile. Chithear na farpaisich a fhuair na prìomh dhuaisean air an telebhisean air BBC Alba agus bidh BBC Radio nan Gàidheal a' craoladh bhon Mhòd gach latha.

VOCABULARY
an Dàmhair (f) - October
gach - each
as motha - biggest
saoghal (m) - world
cruinneachadh (m) - gathering
luchd-labhairt (m, pl) - speakers
a' chiad - the first
còrr is - more than
air ais - back, ago
diofar àite (m) - a different place
fosgladh (m) - opening
oifigeil - official
cuirm-chiùil (f) - concert
a' tighinn gu ceann - coming to an end
còisir (f) - choir
farpais (f) - competition
aithris (f) **bàrdachd** - poetry recitation
sgeulachd (f) - story
litreachas (m) - literature
iomain (f) - shinty

bonn (m) **òir** - gold medal

seinn (f) **aon-neach** - solo singing

as ainmeile - most renowned, most notable

chithear - may be seen

farpaiseach (m) - competitor

fhuair - got

prìomh dhuaisean (f, pl) - main prizes / awards

a' craoladh - broadcasting

COMPREHENSION QUESTIONS

Answer the following questions in English.

1. What two claims are made about the status of the Royal National Mòd?

   _____

   _____

2. When and where was the first National Mòd held?

   _____

   _____

3. How does the Mòd begin?

   _____

   _____

4. Which competitions are the most notable?

 ✎_____

_____

5. What are we told about media coverage of the Mòd?

 ✎_____

_____

* * *

When you've finished, you can find the answers on page 170.

33

ANAGRAM 3
JUMBLED LETTERS

In this anagram challenge, your task is to unscramble the letters of the two anagrams to find the words being described in the definitions. If you need some help, look at the next page to find a hint for each anagram. Then see how many other words in Gaelic (of three or more letters) you can make using the letters from the anagram. **Gur math a thèid leat!**

* * *

I. DEFINITION: **tha am facal seo ag innse gu bheil rudeigin a' dol a thachairt.**

GADOSHIFL

_____ _____

_____ _____

_____ _____

_____ _____

_____ _____

_____ _____

_____   _____
_____   _____
_____   _____
_____   _____
_____   _____

2. DEFINITION: **gheibh thu seo ann an diofar chànanan.**

CERATHISLA

_____   _____
_____   _____
_____   _____
_____   _____
_____   _____
_____   _____
_____   _____
_____   _____
_____   _____
_____   _____

HINTS

1. This will not bring closure.
2. This could be a novel idea.

* * *

When you're ready, turn to page 170 to find the anagram solutions.

34

DÈ 'N AOIS A THA THU?
NUMBER FOCUS

In this activity, we're going to practise numbers in the context of talking about a person's age. Read the explanation below and complete the exercises that follow.

* * *

To ask someone what age they are, you say **dè 'n aois a tha thu?** or **dè 'n aois a tha sibh?** if speaking to an older person or if you're being more formal or polite. To ask about another person's age, you say **dè 'n aois a tha** followed by the person's name or by a pronoun if you're not giving their name. For example: **dè 'n aois a tha Brian?** or **dè 'n aois a tha e / i?** ("how old is he / she?").

To answer, you say **tha mi, tha Brian** or **tha e / i** followed by the number of years. For example, **tha mi dà fhichead** ("I am forty"), **tha Brian leth-cheud sa dhà** ("Brian is fifty-two") or **tha e / i sia (bliadhn') deug** ("he / she is sixteen (years of age)").

Ages beyond 21 can be expressed in two different ways. For example, 23 can be either **fichead (bliadhna) sa trì** or **trì (bliadhna) air fhichead**, while 34 can be **trithead (bliadhna) sa ceithir** or **ceithir (bliadhn') deug air fhichead**.

When giving any age, you can either include **bliadhna** after the first word in the number or leave it out. Just note that we use the singular form **bliadhna** rather than the plural form **bliadhnaichean**.

Now it's time to practise!

EXERCISE 1 - WHAT AGE?

Write down the ages mentioned in the sentences below.

1. **Tha Ciorstaidh sia deug air fhichead a-nis.**

   ✎ _____

2. **Bha Chris ochd bliadhn' deug an-dè.**

   ✎ _____

3. **Bidh i ceithir fichead sa deich an-ath-bhliadhna.**

   ✎ _____

4. **Ghluais an teaghlach dhan bhaile nuair a bha Pàdraig ceithir bliadhn' deug.**

   ✎ _____

5. **Tha mi smaoineachadh gum bi Lisa ceathrad sa còig am-bliadhna.**

   ✎ _____

EXERCISE 2 - TRANSLATE

Translate the following statements about ages into Gaelic.

1. Sally will be thirteen tomorrow.

    ✎ _____

    _____

2. Alasdair is sixty-six today.

    ✎ _____

    _____

3. I will be twenty-seven this year.

    ✎ _____

    _____

4. Oliver was nineteen yesterday.

    ✎ _____

    _____

5. What age is Shona? She is fifty-three.

    ✎ _____

    _____

* * *

Once you're happy with your answers, you can turn to page 172 to check them.

35

CRANACHAN
TASTE BUD TANTALISER

Cranachan is a delicious dessert that often features on restaurant menus in Scotland. It can vary considerably in content and presentation but is easy to make with just a few simple ingredients. Use the vocabulary list provided to help you read through this recipe for **cranachan**, then answer the questions that follow to test your understanding.

* * *

STUTHAN A DHÌTH

120 g min-choirce
450 g uachdar dùbailte
300 g sùbhan-craoibhe
3–4 spàinean bùird de dh'uisge-beatha
2 spàin bùird mil an fhraoich
rud beag siùcair castair

DEASACHADH

1. Sgaoil a-mach a' mhin-choirce air pana fraighigidh tioram agus tostaig e aig teas meadhanach àrd.
2. Crath am pana gus an tionndaidh a' mhin-choirce dath bàn rudeigin coltach ri briosgaid. Bheir seo eadar ceithir is còig mionaidean.
3. Thoir am pana bhàrr an teas agus dòirt a' mhin-choirce air truinnsear gus am fuaraich e nas luaithe.
4. Dèan purée de na sùbhan-craoibhe le bhith a' bruthadh leth dhe na measan agus gan criathradh. Cuir crathadh de shiùcar castair air airson a dhèanamh nas mìlse.
5. Cuir mun cuairt an t-uachdar dùbailte gus am bi e dìreach air seatadh, agus cuir a' mhil agus an t-uisge-beatha na cheann. Thoir an aire nach cuir thu mun cuairt an t-uachdar cus.
6. Blais am measgachadh agus cuir tuilleadh mil no uisge-beatha ris ma tha sin a dhìth.
7. Cuir a' mhin-choirce na cheann agus cuir mun cuairt e gu h-aotrom gus am bi am measgachadh an ìre mhath teann.
8. Cuir sreath mu seach dhen uachdar is de na sùbhan-craoibhe is am purée air muin a chèile ann an soitheachan is leig leis fuarachadh beagan mus ith duin' e.

VOCABULARY

min-choirce (f) - oatmeal
uachdar (m) **dùbailte** - double cream
sùbh-craoibhe (m) - raspberry
spàin-bùird (f) - tablespoon
mil (f) **an fhraoich** - heather honey

rud (m) **beag** - a little

sgaoil - spread

pana (m) **fraighigidh** - frying pan

tostaig - toast

meadhanach àrd - relatively / medium high

crath - shake

gus - until

tionndaidh - turn

rudeigin - something

coltach ri - like, akin to

bheir - will take

eadar - between

airson - in order to

nas mìlse - sweeter

dìreach - just

air seatadh - set

cuir ... na cheann - add ... to it

thoir an aire - take care

cus - too much

blais - taste

tuilleadh - more

a dhìth - required

gu h-aotrom - lightly

an ìre mhath - reasonably, fairly

teann - tight, compacted

sreath (f/m) - row, layer

mu seach - alternate

air muin - on top of

a chèile - each other

soitheach (f/m) - dish

leig leis - let / allow it

mus - before

EXERCISE 1 - TRUE OR FALSE?

Some of the following instructions are correct but others are not. Decide whether each one is true or false by circling **ceart** ("true") or **ceàrr** ("false"), then write a corrected version of the ones that are not right.

1. **Tostaig a' mhin-choirce aig teas àrd.**
   CEART | CEÀRR

   _____

   _____

   _____

2. **Dòirt a' mhin-choirce dhan phana.**
   CEART | CEÀRR

   _____

   _____

   _____

3. **Dèan purée de na sùbhan-craoibhe.**
   CEART | CEÀRR

   _____

   _____

   _____

4. **Cuir mun cuairt an t-uachdar dùbailte.**
   CEART | CEÀRR

   ✎_____

   _____

   _____

5. **Cuir tuilleadh bainne no uisge-beatha ris.**
   CEART | CEÀRR

   ✎_____

   _____

   _____

EXERCISE 2 - COMPREHENSION

Answer the following questions in English.

1. Which ingredients are measured in spoonfuls?

   ✎_____

   _____

2. How long does the toasting process take?

   ✎_____

   _____

3. How do you make the purée sweeter?

   ✎_____

   _____

4. What do you have to be careful not to do?

   ✎_____

   _____

5. What is the very last instruction given?

   ✎_____

   _____

* * *

Once you've finished the exercises, turn to page 172 to check your answers.

36

EADAR-THEANGACHADH 4
TRANSLATION CHALLENGE

Below are some sentences to translate into Gaelic. Have a go
without any help first, then take a look at the hints on the next
page if you need to.

* * *

1. When did you meet them last? A fortnight ago.

    _____

   _____

   _____

2. They usually go abroad on holiday in the autumn.

    _____

   _____

   _____

3. Malik said there weren't many at the meeting last night.

✎ _____

_____

_____

4. We don't know when they'll arrive.

✎ _____

_____

_____

5. Do you remember how to get there? I think so.

✎ _____

_____

_____

HINTS

If you need some help, you may find the following hints useful.

1. Remember that you meet "with" someone.
2. "Usually" translates literally as "it is usual for them".
3. Think carefully about what linking phrase to use to introduce what Malik said.
4. Think carefully about how to translate "when". Also note that the relative future form of the verb is required for "they'll arrive".

5. "Do you remember?" is translated literally as "is there memory at you?".

* * *

When you're happy with your translations, turn to page 173 to find our suggestions.

37

CRAOLADH NA GÀIDHLIG
CULTURAL CONNECTIONS

The following text is about **Craoladh na Gàidhlig**, Gaelic broadcasting. Read through the text using the vocabulary list on the next page to help you with any unfamiliar words. Then answer the comprehension questions that follow. **Siuthad a-nis!**

* * *

Tha a' Ghàidhlig ri cluinntinn agus ri faicinn gach latha air na meadhanan craolaidh. Tha BBC Radio nan Gàidheal a' craoladh phrògraman bho leth-uair an dèidh seachd sa mhadainn gu aon uair deug air an oidhche bho Dhiluain gu Dihaoine. Tha na h-uairean craolaidh nas giorra aig an deireadh-sheachdain. Tha na prògraman telebhisein aig BBC Alba rim faicinn eadar còig uairean feasgar is meadhan-oidhche a h-uile latha. Tha mòran aig nach eil Gàidhlig a' coimhead air BBC Alba, gu sònraichte air prògraman ciùil is spòrs is dràma, agus tha sreath de phrògraman ann cuideachd airson luchd-ionnsachaidh. Tha an t-seirbheis rèidio a' tòiseachadh tron t-seachdain le Aithris na Maidne, prògram le measgachadh de naidheachdan ionadail, nàiseanta is eadar-nàiseanta. Gach Oidhche Haoine eadar sia is naoi uairean, cluinnear Na Dùrachdan, prògram far am bi daoine a' cur dhùrachdan gu càirdean, caraidean is luchd-eòlais ann an Alba, Breatann is thall thairis.

VOCABULARY

craoladh (m) - broadcasting

cluinn - hear

faic - see

na meadhanan (m) - the media

Gàidheal (m) - Gael

nas giorra - shorter

deireadh-seachdain (m) - weekend

rim faicinn - to be seen

a h-uile - every

a' coimhead - watching

gu sònraichte - especially

sreath (f/m) - series

luchd-ionnsachaidh (m, pl) - learners

seirbheis (f) - service

a' tòiseachadh - starting

tron - through the

naidheachd (f) - news

ionadail - local

nàiseanta - national

eadar-nàiseanta - international

eadar - between
cluinnear - can be heard
dùrachd (f) - greeting
caraid (m) - relative, friend
luchd-eòlais (m, pl) - acquaintances
thall thairis - abroad

COMPREHENSION QUESTIONS

Answer the following questions in English.

1. What are we told about weekday broadcasts on BBC Radio nan Gàidheal?

   _____

   _____

2. What is said about weekend broadcasts on BBC Radio nan Gàidheal?

   _____

   _____

3. Why do many non-Gaelic speakers enjoy watching BBC Alba?

   _____

   _____

4. What information is given about the *Aithris na Maidne* radio programme?

5. To whom are greetings sent in the *Na Dùrachdan* programme?

* * *

When you're ready, turn to page 176 to check your answers.

38

ANAGRAM 4
JUMBLED LETTERS

Unscramble the letters of each anagram below to find the word being defined. There is a hint for each anagram on the following page if you need some help. Your second challenge is to find as many Gaelic words as you can (of three or more letters) using the letters from the anagram. **Feuch air!**

* * *

I. DEFINITION: **faodaidh tu seo fhaighinn no a thoirt seachad.**

MOLEACHIR

_____   _____
_____   _____
_____   _____
_____   _____

2. DEFINITION: 's e sgil a tha seo a tha feumail dhan a h-uile duine.

GABHÍSHORD

✎_____   _____
_____   _____
_____   _____
_____   _____
_____   _____
_____   _____
_____   _____
_____   _____
_____   _____
_____   _____

HINTS

1. This is a feminine noun that is sometimes used in names.
2. This word can be a verb or a noun.

* * *

Well done! Once you've unscrambled the anagrams, you can check your answers on page 176.

39

PRÌSEAN
NUMBER FOCUS

In this activity, we're going to focus on **prìsean** ("prices"). Read the explanation below, then complete the exercises that follow. **Feuch ort!**

* * *

There are two ways of asking the price of something in Gaelic. **Dè a' phrìs a tha … ?** followed by the thing you are asking about is one way. The other is to say **dè tha … a' cosg?** with the name of the thing you are asking about going between **tha** and **a' cosg**. The second of these questions asks, "what is … costing?" or "what does … cost?".

To answer **dè a' phrìs a tha … ?**, you can simply give the price or say **tha e / i …** followed by the price. Similarly, you can answer **dè tha … a' cosg?** with simply the price or by saying **tha … a' cosg** followed by the price of the thing being discussed. Here are examples of both question forms:

Dè a' phrìs a tha an tiogaid? Tha an tiogaid deich notaichean.

What price is the ticket? The ticket is ten pounds.

Dè tha am baga a' cosg? Tha am baga a' cosg leth-cheud not.

How much does the bag cost? The bag costs fifty pounds.

Not is "a pound" and **notaichean** are "pounds". **Sgillinn** ("a penny") retains the singular form with multiples of the denomination.

In numbers from **aon deug** (11) to **naoi deug** (19), the word **not, notaichean** or **sgillinn** is inserted between the initial element of the number and the **deug,** which conveys the sense "teen". For example, **ceithir sgillinn deug** is 14p and **còig notaichean deug** is £15.

Prices that involve 99p are translated as **ach sgillinn,** literally "but a penny". For example, **deich notaichean ach sgillinn** is £9.99.

EXERCISE 1 - HIGHEST TO LOWEST

Rank the following prices from highest to lowest, writing them out in numerical figures.

a) **dà not agus leth-cheud sgillinn**
b) **seachd notaichean ach sgillinn**
c) **sia notaichean deug**
d) **ochd sgillinn deug**
e) **ceithir fichead not sa còig**

HIGHEST 1. ✎_____

2. ✎_____

3. ✎_____

4. ✎_____

LOWEST 5. ✎_____

EXERCISE 2 - NUMBERS IN WORDS

Write out in words the prices mentioned in the sentences below.

1. Dè tha e a' cosg? Tha e a' cosg £19.99.

   ✎_____

   _____

2. Dè a' phrìs a tha an dealbh sin? Tha an dealbh £1,000.

   ✎_____

   _____

3. Dè a' phrìs a bha e? Bha e £3.50.

   ✎_____

   _____

4. **Chosg an turas air an trèan £14.**

✎_____

_____

5. **Chosg mi £70 anns a' bhùth.**

✎_____

_____

* * *

Once you're happy with your answers, turn to page 178 to check them.

40

BROT ÈISG SMOCTE
TASTE BUD TANTALISER

Cullen Skink is a distinctively Scottish smoked fish soup (**brot èisg smocte**) named after the village of Cullen on the Moray Firth coast. It appears frequently on the menus of Scottish restaurants specialising in fish dishes. Read the recipe below and use the vocabulary list provided to help you with any unfamiliar words. Then complete the exercises that follow.

* * *

STUTHAN A DHÌTH

1 spàin bùird ìm neo-shaillte
1 uinnean meadhanach mòr
2 bhuntàta meadhanach mòr air an rùsgadh agus an gearradh suas nan ciùbaichean beaga
250 g adag smocte
250 ml bainne
1 spàin bùird peirsill air a' mhìn-ghearradh

DEASACHADH

1. Leagh an t-ìm ann am pana sabhs aig teas meadhanach.
2. Cuir an t-uinnean na cheann agus fraighig son eadar còig is ochd mionaidean ach na leig leis a dhol donn.
3. Cuir am buntàta is 300 ml uisge na cheann agus thoir e dhan ghoil.
4. Ìslich an teas agus leig leis eàrr-bhruich airson eadar deich is còig deug mionaidean.
5. Cuir an adag ann am pana eile is còmhdaich e leis a' bhainne. Bruich e gu socair airson còig mionaidean.
6. Thoir an adag às a' bhainne le spàin le tuill ann a' cumail a' bhainne air leth.
7. Gluais an adag gu truinnsear agus leig leis fuarachadh beagan.
8. Nuair a tha e fuar gu leòr airson beantainn ris, bris suas e na chnapan a' toirt às cnàimh sam bith.
9. Cuir am bainne agus na cnapan adaig anns a' phana leis a' mheasgachadh de bhuntàta agus bruich e airson còig mionaidean eile.
10. Cuir craiteachan peirsill na cheann mus riaraich thu am brot.

VOCABULARY

neo-shaillte - unsalted
uinnean (m) - onion
meadhanach - middling, medium
buntàta (m) - potato
air an rùsgadh - peeled

geàrr - cut

ciùb (m) - cube

adag (f) **smocte** - smoked haddock

peirsill (f) - parsley

pana (m) **sabhs** - saucepan

fraighig - fry

leig leis - allow

donn - brown

thoir - bring, take

goil (f) - boil

ìslich - lower, reduce

eàrr-bhruich - simmer

còmhdaich - cover

bruich - boil, cook

gu socair - gently

tuill (m, pl) - holes

a' cumail - keeping

air leth - separate

gluais - move

truinnsear (m) - plate

fuaraich - cool down

beantainn - touching

cnap (m) - chunk, lump

cnàimh (m) - bone

sam bith - any

craiteachan (m) - sprinkling

mus - before

riaraich - serve

brot (m) - broth, soup

EXERCISE 1 - REORDER

Put the following instructions into the correct order so that they match the directions given in the recipe.

a) Boil the fish gently for five minutes.
b) Move the fish onto a plate.
c) Bring it to the boil.
d) Melt the butter.
e) Don't let the onion brown.

ORDER OF STEPS: ✎_____

EXERCISE 2 - COMPREHENSION

Answer the following questions in English.

1. What are the requirements for the two potatoes in the recipe?

✎_____

_____

2. What do you have to do for 10–15 minutes?

✎_____

_____

3. What instruction is given regarding a spoon?

_____

_____

4. What do you have to do after breaking up the fish?

_____

_____

5. What is the final instruction?

_____

_____

* * *

'S math a rinn thu! You'll find the answers to both exercises on page 179.

21. EADAR-THEANGACHADH 1
Translation Challenge

1. **A bheil thu / sibh fileanta ann an Gàidhlig? Chan eil fhathast ach tha mi ag ionnsachadh.**

EXPLANATION:

- You may remember that **chan eil** is the negative answer to a question beginning with **a bheil?** but in this example it is followed by **fhathast**, meaning "yet" or "still", and is translated as "not" rather than "no".
- You could also say **anns a' Ghàidhlig** (literally "in the Gaelic"), but that is less common.
- The verbal noun **ionnsachadh** is preceded by **ag** because it begins with a vowel.

2. **Is toil le Oliver am baile-mòr ach cha toil leis a' cholaiste.**

EXPLANATION:

- In Lewis and some other dialects, **is caomh** would be used for "likes" and **cha chaomh** for "doesn't like". The translation would then be: **is caomh le Oliver am baile mòr ach cha chaomh leis a' cholaiste.**
- **Baile-mòr** is "a city" while **baile** is "a village" or "a settlement".
- We need to use the definite article ("the" in English) in Gaelic before nouns such as college, school or university. **Colaiste** is usually a feminine noun and the appropriate form of the definite article is therefore **a'**. In some dialects, **colaiste** can be a masculine noun and the definite article would then be **an**.

3. **Tha Amanda a' dol dhan taigh-dhealbh le a caraid a-nochd.**

EXPLANATION:

- There are two ways to translate "going to the cinema". The first, as above, is **a' dol dhan taigh-dhealbh**, using the correct form of the preposition **do**. The second is **a' dol chun an taigh-dhealbh**, using the appropriate form of the preposition **gu**. **Dhan** takes the dative form of the following noun while **chun** takes the genitive form.
- "A friend" is **caraid** and **le caraid** would be "with a friend". "With her friend" is **le a caraid**, but to say "with his friend" you'd need to lenite **caraid**, so it becomes **le a charaid**. **A Charaid Chòir** is often used at the start of letters for "Dear Friend" or "Dear Sir".

4. 'S e neach-ciùil a th' innte. Bidh i a' cluich na fìdhle ann an còmhlan.

EXPLANATION:

- There are two words for "musician" in Gaelic. One is **neach-ciùil** as in the translation above. The alternative is **ceòladair**. **Neach** is "a person" and is gender neutral. It features in occupations such as **neach-lagh** ("a lawyer"), **neach-teagaisg** ("a teacher") and **neach-cunntais** ("an accountant").
- To say what occupation someone has, using the feminine form, you use the expression **'s e … a th' innte**, which literally means "it is a … that is in her". The equivalent in the masculine form is **'s e … a th' ann**. For example, **'s e einnseanair a th' ann** ("he's an engineer").
- Note that a noun following a verbal noun goes into the genitive case. That is why the feminine noun **an fhidheall** ("the fiddle") becomes **na fìdhle** (literally "of the fiddle") after **a' cluich** ("playing").
- The habitual action of playing the fiddle is conveyed by a combination of the future tense of the verb "to be" (**bidh**) and the verbal noun "playing" (**a' cluich**).

5. Chan eil i a' cur an t-sneachda an-dràsta ach tha i glè fhuar.

EXPLANATION:

- **A' cur an t-sneachda** literally means "putting the snow" or "a precipitation of snow". **Sneachda** is a masculine

157

noun and it is in the genitive form after the verbal noun **a' cur**. If you wanted to say "there is no snow just now", you would say **chan eil sneachd' ann an-dràsta**.

- **Glè** is the most common word for "very" and it causes the following adjective to be lenited, as in **glè fhuar** ("very cold"). This would also happen with an alternative word for "very" or "truly", **fìor**. **Fìor mhath** is commonly used to say that something is "very good". **Uabhasach** ("terribly" or "dreadfully") is frequently used colloquially to convey "very". It doesn't cause lenition in the following adjective.

22. SABHAL MÒR OSTAIG
Cultural Connections

1. He bought a large estate in the area and established Sabhal Mòr Ostaig.
2. Short courses for learners.
3. Full-time courses began.
4. Degree courses up to doctorate level.
5. The campus has expanded greatly and the newest building is named after Sir Iain Noble.

23. ANAGRAM 1
Jumbled Letters

1. **Leòdhasach** (m) - a person from Lewis; **Leòdhasach** (adj) – of / from / belonging to Lewis

While there are many words that can be made out of these letters, here are some of the most common ones.

- **ach** - but
- **cas** (f) - foot; leg
- **cas** - steep
- **ceò** (f/m) - mist, fog
- **deò** (f) - breath
- **dha** - to him
- **las** - light
- **asad** - from you
- **cead** (m) - permission
- **ceòl** (m) - music
- **deas** (f) - south
- **deas** - right; ready (to)
- **seòl** (m) - sail
- **casad** (m) - cough
- **dòcha** - likely, probable
- **eòlas** (m) - knowledge
- **seadh** - aye, yes
- **achadh** (m) - a field
- **dòchas** (m) - hope
- **eòlach** - knowledgeable, acquainted with
- **Deasach** (m) - person from South Uist

2. **cluicheadair** (m) - a player

- **air** - on
- **car** (m) - turn, twist; during
- **adha** (m) - liver
- **crac** (f) - chat; crack
- **cuid** - some
- **each** (m) - horse
- **luch** (f) - mouse
- **rach** - go
- **reic** - sell
- **adhar** (m) - sky
- **cadal** (m) - sleep
- **cailc** (f) - chalk
- **cearc** (f) - hen
- **clach** (f) - stone
- **cladh** (m) - cemetery
- **creid** - believe
- **eadar** - between
- **luchd** (m) - a load, cargo
- **caraid** (m) - friend
- **cluich** - play
- **cridhe** (m) - heart
- **darach** (m) - oak
- **cladach** (m) - shore
- **cleachd** - use
- **luideach** - silly

24. DÒIGHEAN CUNNTAIS
Number Focus

EXERCISE 1 - LOWEST TO HIGHEST

1. b) fichead sa h-aon (21)
2. e) ceathrad sa ceithir (44)
3. a) seasgad sa dhà (62)
4. c) seachdad sa h-ochd (78)
5. d) ceithir fichead sa còig (85)

EXERCISE 2 - CONVERT

1. seasgad sa trì (63)
2. ceithir fichead sa naoi deug (99)
3. ceathrad sa seachd (47)
4. trì fichead sa h-ochd (68)
5. ochdad sa sia (86)

25. CLÀR-SIÙCAIR
Taste Bud Tantaliser

EXERCISE 1 - REORDER

ORDER OF STEPS: d), f), b), e), a), c)

EXERCISE 2 - FIND THE GAELIC

1. leig leis seatlaigeadh
2. thoir bhàrr an teas e
3. cuir an fhaoineag na cheann

4. leagh an siùcar gu lèir
5. fhad 's a tha e a' goil
6. rud beag ime

26. EADAR-THEANGACHADH 2
Translation Challenge

1. **Tha mi a' smaoineachadh gu bheil iad a' tighinn madainn a-màireach.**

EXPLANATION:

- The present tense of the verb "to be" is combined with the verbal noun of the verb **smaoinich** to convey the act of thinking.
- To say what someone is thinking, you use the reported speech form (the linking form) of the verb "to be" – **gu bheil** – followed by the verbal noun form of the verb that describes the action, in this case **a' tighinn** ("coming").
- When you want to say "tomorrow morning", the word order is the other way round compared to English, as you put the time of day before "tomorrow", giving us **madainn a-màireach**. It works the same with "tomorrow afternoon / evening", which would be **feasgar a-màireach**.

2. 'S e dealbhaiche a th' ann an Sarah. Tha i ag obair bhon taigh.

EXPLANATION:

- If you've completed some of the other activities in this book, you'll remember that you use the formulation **'s e ... a th' ann / innte** to say what a person's occupation is. When you are naming a particular person, you say **'s e ... a th' ann an** followed by the name. If the person's name begins with **b**, **f**, **m** or **p**, it becomes **'s e ... a th' ann am ....**

- **Bhon taigh** is literally "from the house". You could also say **bhon dachaigh** for "from home", while **aig an taigh** would be "at home".

3. Chunnaic mi prògram math mu dheidhinn sin air an telebhisean a-raoir.

EXPLANATION:

- **Chunnaic** is the past tense positive form of the irregular verb **faic** ("see"). **Chan fhaca** is the negative form ("did not see").

- "A good programme" can be translated as above (**prògram math**) or as **deagh phrògram**. There are only a few adjectives that come before the noun in Gaelic. **Deagh** is one of them. Other common ones are **droch** ("bad") and **seann** ("old"). These adjectives usually lenite the following noun. For example, **droch shìde** ("bad weather") and **seann chòta** ("an old coat").

4. **An robh thu / sibh riamh aig fèis ciùil anns na h-eileanan?**

EXPLANATION:

- To ask a question in the past tense of the verb "to be", you use the interrogative form **an robh?**. This past tense form is used to translate both the simple past ("were / was … ?") and the present perfect ("have you / has he etc. been … ?") in English. A positive answer begins with **bha** while a negative one begins with **cha robh**.
- **Riamh** is used to convey "ever" in a past context. **Gu bràth** and **gu sìorraidh** are used in a future context.
- **Fèis** is the word for "a festival". It is a feminine noun. When you wish to specify "a music festival", it becomes **fèis ciùil**. **Ceòl** is "music" and **ciùil** is the genitive form of the noun.
- An **h-** is used before **eileanan**, as the plural form of **eilean** begins with a vowel and the plural definite article **na** ends in a vowel. It is common practice in Gaelic to separate a word ending in a vowel from the next word beginning with a vowel with forms such as this one.

5. **Bidh am plèan a' laighe air an tràigh ann am Barraigh.**

EXPLANATION:

- There are two examples in this sentence of nouns beginning with **p** or **b**. When you have a masculine noun beginning with either of these letters, the definite article "the" takes the form **am**. The same goes for masculine nouns beginning with **f** or **m**.

- Habitual actions are generally conveyed using the future tense of the verb "to be", followed by the verbal noun form of the verb being used, in this case **a' laighe** ("landing").
- **Tràigh** is a feminine noun, meaning "beach". It is found in place names such as Ballantrae in Ayrshire in Scotland – **Baile na Tràgha**.

27. FÈISEAN
Cultural Connections

1. The first **fèis** was held on Barra.
2. They were concerned that children were not learning about traditional music in formal education in school.
3. They planned to hold a festival in the summer when the schools would be on holiday.
4. A **fèis** lasts for five days and finishes with a ceilidh on the final night.
5. There are 47 **fèisean** across Scotland today and these are attended by around 6,000 youngsters.

28. ANAGRAM 2
Jumbled Letters

1. **naidheachd** (f) - news
   While there are many words that can be made out of these letters, here are some of the most common ones.

   - **ach** - but
   - **can** - say
   - **dha** - to him
   - **dhi** - to her
   - **iad** - they
   - **adha** (m) - liver

- **aice** - at her, hers
- **aidh** - aye, yes
- **cead** (m) - permission
- **each** (m) - horse
- **iadh** - encompass

- **nach** - whom, that ... not
- **cidhe** (m) - quay, pier
- **neach** (m) - person
- **chaidh** - went
- **achadh** (m) - a field

2. **riaraichte** - satisfied

- **ach** - but
- **air** - on
- **car** (m) - turn, twist
- **cat** (m) - cat
- **aire** (f) - heed, attention
- **cath** (m) - battle
- **ciar** - darken; dusky
- **each** (m) - horse
- **rach** - go
- **reic** - sell
- **taic** (f) - support

- **caith** - throw; spend, wear
- **crath** - shake
- **crith** (f) - trembling, shake
- **teich** - flee, escape
- **their** - say
- **cathair** (f) - chair
- **criathar** (m) - sieve; riddle
- **riaraich** - satisfy

29. DÈ 'N UAIR A THA E?
Number Focus

EXERCISE I - WHEN?

1. at 6 o'clock
2. at 2 pm
3. at 7:30
4. about 11 o'clock
5. at 9 am on Thursday

EXERCISE 2 - ADD THE TIME

1. Bidh an t-aiseag a' ruighinn an eilein aig **còig uairean feasgar.**

   TRANSLATION: *The ferry reaches the island at 5 pm.*

2. Chì mi thu aig an stèisean aig **leth-uair an dèidh deich.**

   TRANSLATION: *I'll see you at the station at 10:30.*

3. Cha bhi mi a-staigh gu **ochd uairean feasgar.**

   TRANSLATION: *I won't be in until 8 pm.*

4. Tha prògram math air an rèidio a-nochd aig **leth-uair an dèidh naoi.**

   TRANSLATION: *There's a good programme on the radio tonight at 9:30.*

5. Feumaidh sinn falbh aig **leth-uair an dèidh sia sa mhadainn.**

   TRANSLATION: *We'll have to leave at 6:30 am.*

30. ARAN-MILIS
Taste Bud Tantaliser

EXERCISE 1 - COMPREHENSION

1. To grease the baking tin.
2. In a mixing bowl.
3. Make even rows of fork pricks on the surface.
4. About an hour and a half.
5. About ten minutes.

EXERCISE 2 - FIND THE GAELIC

1. bruich e ann an àmhainn
2. dustaig e le crathadh de shiùcar castair
3. criathraich am flùr
4. fàg e san treidhe gus am fàs e fuar
5. suath a-steach e le do mheuran

31. EADAR-THEANGACHADH 3
Translation Challenge

1. Dè / Cò am fear a tha thu ag iarraidh? An seann fhear no am fear ùr?

OR

Dè / Cò an tè a tha thu ag iarraidh? An t-seann tè no an tè ùr.

EXPLANATION:

- "Which?" can be translated as dè? or cò?
- Am fear refers to "one" when the item is a masculine noun, while an tè refers to "one" when the item is a feminine noun.
- You can use either thu or sibh for "you" as the English sentence does not indicate whether it is an informal or formal / plural "you".
- Seann is one of the few adjectives that precede the noun and it usually causes lenition of the noun. Because seann ends in a double n, a following noun beginning with d, t or s is not lenited.

2. **Is toil / caomh leatha sineubhar ach is fheàrr leis-san uisge-beatha.**

EXPLANATION:

- Most dialects use **is toil** for "likes", but in Lewis and certain other dialects **is caomh** is used.
- To indicate who it is that likes something, the appropriate form of the preposition **le** is used after **is toil / is caomh**. "She likes" is, therefore, **is toil / caomh leatha**, which literally means "it is liked by her".
- Similarly, "he prefers" is **is fheàrr leis**, which literally means "it is preferred by him".
- Here, because we're comparing two people, we use **leis-san** for emphasis. If the second half of the sentence were talking about what *she* prefers, it would be **leatha-se**.

3. **An do choinnich / thachair sibh riutha fhathast? Cha do choinnich / thachair.**

EXPLANATION:

- The interrogative or question form of regular past tense verbs is formed by putting **an do?** before the past tense form of the verb, as in **an do choinnich thu?** ("have you met?" or "did you meet?").
- The verbs **coinnich** and **tachair** both mean "meet" and both are followed by the appropriate form of the prepositional pronoun **ri. Riutha** is the third person plural form of **ri** and indicates "they" or "them".
- You can use either **thu** or **sibh** for "you".

4. **Tha sinn an dòchas / dùil sin a dhèanamh uaireigin an-ath-bhliadhna.**

EXPLANATION:

- You translate "we hope" as "we are hoping" – **tha sinn an dòchas** (literally "we are in hope"). "We intend" would be translated in a similar way – **tha sinn an dùil** (literally "we are in expectation").
- To say what you are going to do, you put the noun or pronoun before the verb. This is why we have **sin** ("that") before **a dhèanamh** ("to do"). Other examples would be **an doras a dhùnadh** ("to close the door") and **litir a sgrìobhadh** ("to write a letter").
- Notice that "next year" (**an-ath-bhliadhna**) is hyphenated, while "the next year" (**an ath bhliadhna**) would not be.

5. **Càit a bheil thu airson a dhol às dèidh na dinneir?**
OR

Càit a bheil thu ag iarraidh a dhol às dèidh na dinneir?

EXPLANATION:

- "Want" can be translated by **airson** ("for") or by **ag iarraidh** ("asking (for)"). **Càit a bheil thu airson a dhol?** is literally "where are you for going?", while **càit a bheil thu ag iarraidh a dhol?** is literally "where are you asking to go?".
- **Às dèidh** is a prepositional phrase that needs to be followed by the genitive case of the following noun. Because **dinnear** is a feminine noun, its genitive form **dinneir** is preceded by **na**.

32. AM MÒD NÀISEANTA RÌOGHAIL
Cultural Connections

1. It is the biggest festival in the Gaelic world and it is the largest gathering of Gaelic speakers during the year.
2. The first National Mòd was held in Oban over a hundred years ago.
3. It begins on a Friday with an official opening and a concert.
4. The Gold Medal competitions for solo singing are the most renowned.
5. The winners of the main competitions appear on television on BBC Alba and in BBC Radio nan Gàidheal broadcasts from the Mòd each day.

33. ANAGRAM 3
Jumbled Letters

1. **fosglaidh** - will open
   While there are many words that can be made out of these letters, here are some of the most common ones.

   - **aog** (m) - death
   - **aol** (m) - lime
   - **gas** (m) - gas
   - **iad** - they
   - **lag** (f) - hollow; dent
   - **lag** - weak, feeble, slight
   - **ola** (f) - oil
   - **aois** (f) - age
   - **gaol** (m) - love
   - **glas** (f) - lock
   - **glas** - grey; green
   - **iasg** (m) - fish
   - **lagh** (m) - law
   - **ogha** (m) - grandchild
   - **osag** (f) - breeze, gust

- **goilf** (m) - golf
- **laigh** - lie down
- **glaodh** (m) - call, shout

2. **litreachas** (m) - literature

- **ach** - but
- **ait** - joyful; funny
- **ath** - next
- **ear** (f) - east
- **eas** (m) - waterfall
- **iar** (f) - west
- **ite** (f) - feather
- **ith** - eat
- **ris** - to him
- **sia** - six
- **sil** - rain, drip
- **tha** - is, am, are
- **each** (m) - horse
- **eala** (f) - swan
- **leth** (m) - half
- **lite** (f) - porridge
- **rach** - go
- **reic** - sell
- **sear** - east
- **seat** - set
- **siar** - west
- **taic** (f) - support
- **tais** - damp, moist
- **teas** (m) - heat

- **glaodh** - glue
- **iodhal** (m) - idol

- **thar** - across, over
- **tric** - often, frequent
- **astar** (m) - distance; speed
- **latha** (m) - day
- **liath** - grey, blue grey
- **rithe** - to her
- **srath** (m) - wide valley
- **their** - will say
- **treas** - third
- **treis** (f) - a while
- **athair** (m) - father
- **eathar** (f/m) - boat
- **lasair** (f) - flame
- **leatha** - with / by her
- **salach** - dirty
- **sreath** (f/m) - row, series
- **salaich** - dirty, soil
- **tachair** - happen; meet
- **riaslach** - hectic, in a tizzy

34. DÈ 'N AOIS A THA THU?
Number Focus

EXERCISE 1 - WHAT AGE?

1. Kirsty is 36 now.
2. Chris was 18 yesterday.
3. She'll be 90 next year.
4. The family moved to the town when Patrick was 14.
5. I think Lisa will be 45 this year.

EXERCISE 2 - TRANSLATE

1. **Bidh Sally trì (bliadhn') deug a-màireach.**
2. **Tha Alasdair seasgad / trì fichead sa sia an-diugh.**
3. **Bidh mi fichead sa seachd / seachd air fhichead am-bliadhna.**
4. **Bha Oliver naoi bliadhn' deug an-dè.**
5. **Dè 'n aois a tha Shona? Tha i leth-cheud sa trì. / Tha i dà fhichead sa trì-deug.**

35. CRANACHAN
Taste Bud Tantaliser

EXERCISE 1 - TRUE OR FALSE?

1. Ceàrr - Tostaig a' mhin-choirce aig teas **meadhanach** àrd.
2. Ceàrr - Dòirt a' mhin-choirce **air truinnsear.**
3. Ceart.
4. Ceart.
5. Ceàrr - Cuir tuilleadh **mil** no uisge-beatha ris.

1. The whisky and the honey.
2. It takes four to five minutes.
3. By adding a little caster sugar.
4. Not stir the cream too much.
5. Let the cranachan cool down a bit before anyone eats it.

36. EADAR-THEANGACHADH 4
Translation Challenge

1. **Cuin a choinnich thu riutha mu dheireadh? Cola-deug air ais.**

EXPLANATION:

- You can use either the verb **coinnich** or **tachair** for "meet", but both have to be followed by the appropriate form of the preposition **ri.** In this instance, it is the third person plural form of the prepositional pronoun **riutha** ("with them").
- You can use either **thu** or **sibh** for "you" as the English question does not specify whether it is an informal or formal / plural "you".
- **Mu dheireadh** has various meanings, including "last" (like in this sentence), "eventually", "finally" and "at last". "At long last" is **mu dheireadh thall.**
- The word **cola-deug** for fortnight is derived from **ceithir latha deug** ("fourteen days", literally "four days teen").

2. **Is àbhaist dhaibh a bhith a' dol a-null thairis air làithean-saora as t-Fhoghar.**

EXPLANATION:

- **Is àbhaist do** is the phrase that is used to convey the sense of "usually". The preposition **do** can be followed by a person's name – for example in **is àbhaist do Dhaibhidh ...** ("David usually ...") – or **do** changes into the appropriate form of the prepositional pronoun as in **dhaibh** ("to them").
- The phrase **is àbhaist do** is often followed by **a bhith**, "to be". In this sentence, the literal translation would be "it is usual for them to be going".
- **A-null thairis** is used when there is movement involved. The state of being "abroad" or "overseas" is **thall thairis**.
- "In autumn / fall" can be translated as **anns an Fhoghar** or as **as t-Fhoghar**, as above.

3. **Thuirt Malik nach robh mòran aig a' choinneimh a-raoir.**

EXPLANATION:

- **Thuirt** ("said") is the past tense form of the irregular verb **abair** ("say"). The alternative form **thubhairt** is used when giving emphasis to the word.
- When reporting what someone said about something that happened, we need to choose between **gun robh** and **nach robh** to begin the second clause involving the verb "to be". It should begin with **gun robh** if the statement about the past event is positive, and with **nach robh** if it is negative, as in our sentence above.

- **Coinneamh** is a feminine noun which goes into the dative form after a preposition. **Aig coinneimh** would be "at a meeting", while **aig a' choinneimh** means "at the meeting".

4. **Chan eil fhios againn cuin a ruigeas iad.**

EXPLANATION:

- **Fios** is the word for "knowledge" and **tha fios / fhios agam** is the phrase "I know". It literally means "there is knowledge at me". The prepositional pronoun changes to reflect the person being spoken about. In this sentence it changes to **againn** (literally "at us"), therefore conveying the idea of "we know".
- Notice that the question form **cuin** is used for "when", rather than **nuair**.
- **Ruigeas** is the relative future form of the irregular verb **ruig** ("arrive" or "reach").

5. **A bheil cuimhn' agad ciamar a gheibh thu ann? Tha mi a' smaoineachadh gu bheil.**

EXPLANATION:

- To say "I remember" (**tha cuimhn' agam**) you use a very similar construction to "I know" in our previous sentence. **Tha cuimhn' agam** literally means "there is memory at me". The prepositional pronoun based on **aig** changes form depending on the person being referred to. That is why you get **a bheil cuimhn' agad?** which literally means "is there memory at you?".

175

- If you were asking this question formally, to a group of people, to someone older or to someone in authority, you would use **agaibh** instead of **agad** – **a bheil cuimhn' agaibh?**.
- You can use the question word **ciamar** or **mar** for "how" in this sentence.
- **Gheibh** is the future tense of the irregular verb **faigh** ("get").
- "I think so" is translated literally as "I am thinking" followed by the positive form of the linking verb "to be" (**gu bheil**), literally meaning "that (it) is".

37. CRAOLADH NA GÀIDHLIG
Cultural Connections

1. Broadcasts begin at 7:30 am and finish at 11 pm.
2. The broadcast hours are shorter.
3. Many non-Gaelic speakers tune into BBC Alba particularly for music, sports and drama programmes.
4. It has a mix of local, national and international news.
5. Greetings are sent to relatives, friends and acquaintances in Scotland, Britain and abroad.

38. ANAGRAM 4
Jumbled Letters

1. **comhairle** (f) - advice, counsel; council
   While there are many words that can be made out of these letters, here are some of the most common ones:

- **ach** - but
- **air** - on
- **aol** (m) - lime
- **arm** (m) - army
- **car** (m) - turn, twist
- **cor** (m) - condition, state
- **ear** (f) - east
- **iar** (f) - west
- **mac** (m) - son
- **mar** - as, like
- **mil** (f) - honey
- **och!** - alas!
- **oir** (f/m) - edge
- **olc** (m) - evil
- **orm** - on me
- **aice** - at her, hers
- **aire** (f) - attention
- **caol** (m) - kyle, sound
- **caol** - thin
- **ciar** - dusky

- **crom** - bent, bend
- **each** (m) - horse
- **lach** (f) - wild duck
- **leam** - with me
- **loch** (f/m) - loch
- **mach** - out, outwards
- **mair** - last
- **maol** - blunt; bald
- **mear** - merry
- **mial** (f) - louse, tick
- **moch** - early
- **rach** - go
- **caomh** - like; tender, gentle
- **coire** (m) - kettle
- **craol** - broadcast
- **laoch** (m) - warrior, hero
- **riamh** - ever
- **roimhe** - before

2. **sgrìobhadh** - writing

- **bad** (m) - spot
- **bha** - was, were
- **bho** - from; since
- **bìd** - bite
- **bog** - soft; wet
- **gar** - warm, heat
- **gas** (m) - gas

- **rag** - stiff, unbending
- **sad** - throw
- **bìog** (f) - chirp, squeak
- **brag** (m) - crack, bang
- **daor** - dear
- **gabh** - take
- **grad** - sudden, quick

- **grod** - rot; rotten
- **ogha** (m) - grandchild
- **osag** (f) - breeze, gust
- **rìgh** (m) - king
- **robh** - was, were
- **saor** (m) - joiner
- **saor** - cheap; free
- **sgar** - separate
- **sìor** - ever, always
- **bogsa** (m) - box; accordion
- **doras** (m) - door
- **dragh** (m) - bother, trouble; pull
- **garbh** - rough, coarse
- **bodhar** - deaf
- **sgrìob** (f) - scrape
- **sgrìobh** - write

39. PRÌSEAN
Number Focus

EXERCISE 1 - HIGHEST TO LOWEST

1. e) £85
2. c) £16
3. b) £6.99
4. a) £2.50
5. d) £0.18

EXERCISE 2 - NUMBERS IN WORDS

1. fichead not ach sgillinn
2. mìle not
3. trì notaichean agus leth-cheud sgillinn
4. ceithir notaichean deug
5. seachdad not / trì fichead not sa deich

40. BROT ÈISG SMOCTE
Taste Bud Tantaliser

EXERCISE 1 - REORDER

ORDER OF STEPS: d), e), c), a), b)

EXERCISE 2 - COMPREHENSION

1. They must be reasonably big / medium-sized, be peeled and cut into small cubes.
2. Lower the heat and let it simmer.
3. Take the haddock out of the milk with a draining spoon.
4. Make sure any bones are removed.
5. Add a sprinkling of parsley before you serve the soup.

15-MINUTE COFFEE BREAKS

CHECKLIST
15-MINUTE COFFEE BREAKS

Reading Focus
- ❏ Ceap Breatainn - page 184
- ❏ Uisge-beatha - page 201
- ❏ An Clò Mòr - page 216

Grammar Focus
- ❏ An tràth caithte - page 189
- ❏ An tràth teachdail - page 206
- ❏ Ainmearan gnìomhaireach 1 - page 221
- ❏ Ainmearan gnìomhaireach 2: a' dol - page 233

Vocabulary Consolidation
- ❏ Siubhal - page 195
- ❏ Dreuchdan - page 212
- ❏ Slàinte - page 228

41

CEAP BREATAINN
READING FOCUS

The text below is about the island of Cape Breton in Canada. Read the text as many times as you need to, using the vocabulary list to help you, then have a go at the comprehension and language exercises that follow.

* * *

'S e eilean a th' ann an Ceap Breatainn air taobh sear Chanada. Tha an t-eilean 110 mìle de dh'fhaid agus mu 75 mìle de leud agus tha mu 132,000 neach a' fuireach ann. Tha cabhsair a' ceangal an eilein ri tìr-mòr Alba Nuaidh. Chì thu àiteachan air feadh an eilein le ainmean Albannach agus coinnichidh tu ri daoine gu leòr le ainmean Gàidhealach bho Alba. Chaidh na ceudan dhaoine à Gàidhealtachd na h-Alba gu Canada san naoidheamh linn deug agus sheatlaig mòran dhiubh ann an Ceap Breatainn. Bha faisg air 100,000 neach ann an Alba Nuadh aig an robh Gàidhlig ann an 1850. Chan eil ach mu 2,000 neach aig a bheil Gàidhlig an-diugh ach tha daoine òga a' gabhail ùidh sa chànan is san dualchas agus tha cuid dhiubh ag ionnsachadh Gàidhlig. Tha Colaiste Gàidhlig ann an St Anne's a tha a' teagasg a' chànain agus a' ruith chlasaichean ann am fidhlearachd, pìobaireachd, òrain luaidh is dannsa ceum am measg eile. Dh'fhosgail bun-sgoil Ghàidhlig ann am Mabù ann an 2021 is tha cùrsaichean Gàidhlig is mun chànan rim faighinn aig oilthigh air an eilean is air tìr-mòr Alba Nuaidh faisg air an eilean.

VOCABULARY

taobh (m) **sear** - east side
mìle (f/m) - mile; thousand
fad (m) - length
leud (m) - width, breadth
cabhsair (m) - causeway; pavement
ceangail - connect, tie
tìr-mòr (m) - mainland
Alba Nuadh (f) - Nova Scotia
chì - will see
air feadh - throughout
Gàidhealtachd (f) - Highlands
linn (f/m) - century
seatlaig - settle
dhiubh - of them
gabh ùidh - take an interest
dualchas (m) - heritage
teagaisg - teach
fidhlearachd (f) - fiddling
pìobaireachd (f) - piping
òrain (m, pl) **luaidh** - waulking songs
dannsa (m) **ceum** - step dancing

bun-sgoil (f) - primary school
cùrsa (m/f) - course
rim faighinn - to be had
oilthigh (m) - university

EXERCISE 1 - COMPREHENSION

Answer the following questions in English.

1. What size is the island?

   ✎_____

   _____

2. What is said about the Scottish influence on the island?

   ✎_____

   _____

3. What is the reason for the Scottish influence?

   ✎_____

   _____

4. What information is given about the number of Gaelic
   speakers historically and today?

   ✎_____

   _____

5. What is provided at the Gaelic College in St Anne's?

   ✎_____

   _____

EXERCISE 2 - WRITE THE NUMBERS

The numbers below appear in the text. Write out each phrase in full in Gaelic, giving the numbers in words.

1. 75 miles

   _____

2. 132,000 people

   _____

3. 100,000 people

   _____

4. the year 1850

   _____

5. 2,000 people

   _____

EXERCISE 3 - FIND THE GAELIC

Find the Gaelic in the text for the following words or phrases.

1. the mainland of Nova Scotia

   _____

2. you'll meet plenty of people

   _____

3. in the nineteenth century

  ✎_____

4. some of them are learning Gaelic

  ✎_____

5. a Gaelic primary school opened

  ✎_____

* * *

Once you've finished, turn to page 239 to check your answers.

42

AN TRÀTH CAITHTE
GRAMMAR FOCUS

In this Grammar Focus, we're going to practise using the past tense of regular verbs in Gaelic. Read the explanation below, then put this into practice by completing the exercises that follow. **Siuthad a-nis!**

* * *

FORMING THE PAST TENSE

In Gaelic, the root form of the verb is the imperative or command form: for example, **suidh** ("sit") or **dùin** ("shut / close"). The past tense of the verb is normally formed by leniting the first letter of the root. This is shown in writing by inserting an **h** as the second letter of the verb. (This is similar to what we've seen with certain adjectives in the Mini Grammar Challenge, Activity 2, "**Buadhairean**", on page 8). For example:

seas *stand* becomes **sheas** *stood*

bris *break* becomes **bhris** *broke*

However, certain letters do not show lenition in writing and they retain the same form as the root in the past tense. These letters are **l, n, r** and the combinations **sg, sm, sp** and **st**. For example:

leum *jump* remains as **leum** *jumped*

ruith *run* remains as **ruith** *ran*

stad *stop* remains as **stad** *stopped*

If a verb begins with a vowel, the past tense is formed by placing **dh'** before the root of the verb. For example:

òl *drink* becomes **dh'òl** *drank*

ith *eat* becomes **dh'ith** *ate*

When a verb begins with **f** followed by a vowel, it is lenited and **dh'** is placed before it. This is because the combination **fh** is generally not pronounced and therefore the verb is treated as beginning with a vowel. For example:

fosgail *open* becomes **dh'fhosgail** *opened*

THE PAST TENSE NEGATIVE FORM

In all cases, the negative of the past tense is formed by placing **cha do** before the positive form (of the past tense). For example:

shuidh *sat* becomes **cha do shuidh** *did not sit*

dh'obraich *worked* becomes **cha do dh'obraich** *did not work*

THE PAST TENSE QUESTION FORM

The interrogative or question form of the past tense of regular verbs is formed in a similar way, by placing **an do** before the positive form. For example:

dhùin *shut* becomes **an do dhùin?** *did ... shut?*

dh'fhaighnich *asked* becomes **an do dh'fhaighnich?** *did ... ask?*

To answer a past tense question, you use either the positive or the negative form of the verb as appropriate. For example:

— **An do thuig thu?**
— **Thuig.**
— *Did you understand?*
— *Yes.*

— **An do dh'fhalbh i?**
— **Cha do dh'fhalbh.**
— *Did she leave?*
— *No.*

Thusa nis! Now it's over to you to practise on the following page.

EXERCISE 1 - FILL IN THE GAPS

Fill in the blanks in the following sentences with the right form of the verb.

1. **gabh** *take* becomes ✎_____ *took*
2. **lìon** *fill* becomes ✎_____ *filled*
3. **fòn** *phone* becomes ✎_____
   phoned
4. **cluich** *play* becomes ✎_____
   did not play
5. **èist** *listen* becomes ✎_____
   did not listen
6. **pàigh** *pay* becomes ✎_____
   did ... pay?
7. **sgrìobh** *write* becomes ✎_____
   did ... write?

EXERCISE 2 - COMPLETE THE SENTENCES

Complete the following sentences with the correct form of the verb given in brackets so that the Gaelic sentence matches the English translation. We've done the first one for you as an example.

An do ghlan thu am bòrd? **(glan)**
TRANSLATION: *Did you clean the table?*

1. ✎_____ Sheila aig a' chèilidh.
   (seinn)
   TRANSLATION: *Sheila sang at the ceilidh.*

2. ✎_____ iad fhathast. (till)

TRANSLATION: *They haven't returned yet.*

3. ✎_____ sibh tràth? (èirich)

TRANSLATION: *Did you get up early?*

4. ✎_____ mi an leabhar sin. (leugh)

TRANSLATION: *I haven't read that book.*

5. ✎_____ Calum na soithichean.
   (nigh)

TRANSLATION: *Calum washed the dishes.*

6. Cuin a ✎_____ an trèan
   Glaschu? (fàg)

TRANSLATION: *When did the train leave Glasgow?*

EXERCISE 3 - REARRANGE

Sort the words in these sentences into the correct order so that
they make sense. Then translate each sentence into English.

1. dhùin | geata | do | iad | an | cha

✎_____

_____

_____

2. biadh | do | sibh | ghabh | san | an | taigh-òsta

✎_____

_____

_____

3. sinn | an | faisg | air | shuidh | uinneig

_____

_____

4. thu | do | siùcar | a' | chuir | chofaidh | an | anns

_____

_____

5. am | càr | stad | an | dubh | poileas

_____

_____

6. i | bhris | agus | cas | i | thuit | a

_____

_____

_____

* * *

Once you've finished, you can find the answers on page 240.

43

SIUBHAL
VOCABULARY CONSOLIDATION

In this activity, we're going to practise some vocabulary on the topic of travel. We have chosen 20 words or phrases on this topic and have put together some exercises which will help you to familiarise yourself with this vocabulary. Read through the list a few times, then cover it up with your hand or a piece of paper and try to complete the exercises that follow without looking. **Feuch ort!**

* * *

a' fàgail - leaving, departing
a' ruighinn - arriving, reaching
dòighean (f, pl) **siubhail** - modes of transport
ceangal (m) - connection
ionad (m) **luchd-turais** - tourist office
làrach-lìn (f/m) - website
a' lorg àite-fuirich - finding a place to stay
a' fuireach ann an taigh-òsta - staying in a hotel
a' gabhail taigh air mhàl - renting a house

a' dol air làithean-saora - going on holiday
stèisean (m) **thrèanaichean** - train station
aiseag (m) - ferry
port-adhair (m) - airport
tiogaid (f) **siubhail** - travel ticket
cead-siubhail (m) - passport
a' **dol cuairt** - taking a trip / tour
a' **togail dhealbhan** - taking photographs
air chall - lost
clàr-siubhail (m) - itinerary
a' **pacaigeadh baga** - packing a bag

EXERCISE 1 - TRANSLATE

Write the Gaelic translation of these words or phrases. Try not
to refer back to the list.

1. modes of transport

   ✎_____

2. passport

   ✎_____

3. lost

   ✎_____

4. arriving

   ✎_____

5. staying in a hotel

   ✎_____

EXERCISE 2 - WHAT'S MISSING?

1. Take another look at the five words and phrases in the following list.

> **port-adhair**
> **a' fàgail**
> **ceangal**
> **a' lorg àite-fuirich**
> **a' togail dhealbhan**

Now, cover up the list above with your hand or a piece of paper and complete the list below with the one that's missing.

> **a' lorg àite-fuirich**
> **ceangal**
> **a' togail dhealbhan**
> **port-adhair**

> ✎ _____

2. Let's do the same with another five words and phrases in the list.

> **aiseag**
> **stèisean thrèanaichean**
> **a' pacaigeadh baga**
> **làrach-lìn**
> **a' gabhail taigh air mhàl**

Now cover them up and spot what's missing from the following list.

a' gabhail taigh air mhàl
làrach-lìn
a' pacaigeadh baga
stèisean thrèanaichean

✎ _____

3. Here are the next five.

a' lorg àite-fuirich
a' ruighinn
clàr-siubhail
dòighean siubhail
ionad luchd-turais

Which one is missing from the following list?

ionad luchd-turais
dòighean siubhail
a' lorg àite-fuirich
a' ruighinn

✎ _____

4. Here is the next list of five pieces of vocabulary.

tiogaid siubhail
a' dol air làithean-saora
a' dol cuairt
cead-siubhail
air chall

Cover them up and write down the missing word or phrase.

cead-siubhail

air chall

a' dol air làithean-saora

tiogaid siubhail

_____

EXERCISE 3 - ODD ONE OUT

1. Which *two* of the words and phrases from the list below would you be unlikely to use when talking about travelling for work?

   làrach-lìn

   a' dol air làithean-saora

   a' fuireach ann an taigh-òsta

   ionad luchd-turais

   cead-siubhail

   _____

   _____

2. Which *four* of the following words or phrases would you be unlikely to use if you were driving to stay with friends in your own country?

   clàr-siubhail

   stèisean thrèanaichean

   a' gabhail taigh air mhàl

   port-adhair

   air chall

   a' lorg àite-fuirich

✎_____

✎_____

✎_____

✎_____

EXERCISE 4 - FILL IN THE GAPS

Fill in each gap with the most appropriate word or phrase from the vocabulary list.

1. Gheibh thu fiosrachadh mu cheanglaichean aig an ionad ✎_____.

2. Tha ✎_____ eadar-dhealaichte eadar Inbhir Nis agus Glaschu.

3. Feumaidh tu ✎_____ airson a dhol a-null thairis.

4. Bu chòir dhut coimhead air an ✎_____ airson fios mu thaigh-òsta.

5. Is toil leinn a bhith ✎_____ anns a' phàirc.

* * *

'S math a rinn thu! Now it's time to check your answers on page 241.

44

UISGE-BEATHA
READING FOCUS

In the text below, you'll learn more about **uisge-beatha** ("whisky"), one of Scotland's most famous exports. Read the text and answer the comprehension and language questions that follow to test your understanding.

* * *

Tha uisge-beatha na h-Alba ainmeil air feadh an t-saoghail agus tha fèill mhòr air a-nis ann an iomadh dùthaich. Tha am facal *uisge-beatha* a' ciallachadh an aon rud ri *aqua vitae* ann an Laideann agus tha am facal Beurla *whisky* bonntaichte air an fhacal Gàidhlig *uisge*. Tha uisge-beatha air a bhith air a dhèanamh ann an Alba o chionn iomadh linn. An-diugh, tha uisge-beatha air a dhèanamh ann an còrr is ceud gu leth taigh-staile ann an diofar sgìrean dhen dùthaich. 'S e Srath Spè an sgìre as ainmeile airson uisge-beatha is tha am facal gleann a' nochdadh tric ann an ainmean an uisge-bheatha san sgìre sin. Tha eilean Ìle cuideachd aithnichte airson uisge-beatha le deich taighean-staile ainmeil agus blas sònraichte na mòine air an uisge-bheatha. Gheibhear uisge-beatha ann am mòran eileanan eile bho Arcaibh sìos gu Arainn agus tha taighean-staile ùra rim faighinn ann an eileanan mar Na Hearadh, Ratharsair, Tiriodh is Uibhist.

VOCABULARY
ainmeil - famous
air feadh - throughout
saoghal (m) - world
fèill (f) - demand, market
iomadh - many
dùthaich (f) - country
facal (m) - word
Laideann (f) - Latin
bonntaichte air - based on
o chionn - since
linn (f/m) - century
còrr is - more than
taigh-staile (m) - distillery
diofar - different
sgìre (f) - area, district
Srath Spè (m) - Strathspey
gleann (m) - glen
nochd - appear
tric - often
Ìle - Islay
aithnichte - known, recognised
blas (m) - flavour, taste

sònraichte - special
mòine (f) - peat
gheibhear - can be found
Arcaibh - Orkney
Arainn - Arran
Na Hearadh - Harris
Ratharsair - Raasay
Tiriodh - Tiree
Uibhist - Uist

EXERCISE 1 - COMPREHENSION

Answer the following questions in English.

1. What are we told about the market for Scotch whisky?

   ✎ _____

   _____

2. What linguistic connections are made in the text?

   ✎ _____

   _____

3. How many distilleries are there in Scotland?

   ✎ _____

   _____

4. What information is given about the Strathspey area?

   ✎ _____

   _____

5. How is Islay whisky distinctive?

✎ _____

_____

EXERCISE 2 - MATCH THE PHRASES

Draw a line to match each Gaelic phrase to its correct English translation.

GAELIC		ENGLISH	
1.	a' ciallachadh an aon rud	A.	*it's in great demand*
2.	rim faighinn	B.	*for many centuries*
3.	o chionn iomadh linn	C.	*appears often*
4.	tha fèill mhòr air	D.	*meaning the same (thing)*
5.	a' nochdadh tric	E.	*to be found*

EXERCISE 3 - FIND THE WORDS

1. Name four words in the text that are connected with divisions of land.

✎ _____

_____

2. There are three nouns that appear in both their singular and plural form in the text. Identify them and write down both forms of each.

✎ _____

_____

3. Name three words in the text that refer to time.

✎_____

_____

4. List five words or phrases that refer to number or incidence in the text.

✎_____

_____

5. There is one example in the text of the plural form of an adjective. Can you identify it?

✎_____

_____

* * *

Once you've had a go, you can check your answers on page 243.

45

AN TRÀTH TEACHDAIL

GRAMMAR FOCUS

In this Grammar Focus, we're going to practise using the future tense of regular verbs in Gaelic. Read the explanation below, then put this into practice by completing the exercises that follow.

* * *

FORMING THE FUTURE TENSE

If you've already completed Activity 42, "**An tràth caithte**", about the past tense of regular verbs, you may remember that the root form of the verb is the imperative or command form: for example, **tog** ("lift") or **èist** ("listen"). The future tense of the verb is normally formed by adding **-aidh** or **-idh** to the root. If the last vowel in the root is **a**, **o** or **u**, you add **-aidh** to it. If the last vowel in the root is **e** or **i**, you add **-idh**. For example:

stad *stop* becomes **stadaidh** *will stop*

tilg *throw* becomes **tilgidh** *will throw*

fuirich *wait / stay* becomes **fuirichidh** *will wait / will stay*

When a verb root has two syllables and an **-aidh** or **-idh** future tense element is added, it may be contracted so that it is easier to say and remains disyllabic. For example:

tadhail *call (on) / visit* becomes **tadhlaidh** *will call (on) / will visit* (rather than **tadhailidh**)

freagair *answer* becomes **freagraidh** *will answer* (rather than **freagairidh**)

FUTURE TENSE NEGATIVE FORMS

The negative of the future tense is formed by placing **cha** or **chan** before the root form. **Chan** is used before root forms beginning with a vowel or with **f** followed by a vowel. **Cha** lenites the root of the verb. For example:

suidh *sit* becomes **cha shuidh** *will not sit*

ith *eat* becomes **chan ith** *will not eat*

fuirich *wait / stay* becomes **chan fhuirich** *will not wait / will not stay*

FUTURE TENSE QUESTION FORMS

The interrogative or question form of the future tense of regular verbs is formed in a similar way by placing **an** or **am** before the root form. **Am** is used before verb roots beginning with **b, f, m** or **p**. For example:

dùin *shut* becomes **an dùin?** *will ... shut?*

òl *drink* becomes **an òl?** *will ... drink?*

faighnich *ask* becomes **am faighnich?** *will ... ask?*

To answer a question in the future tense, you use either the positive or the negative form of the verb (in the future tense), as appropriate. For example:

— **An coisich sinn?**
— **Coisichidh.**
— *Will we walk?*
— *Yes.*

— **An tuig iad?**
— **Tuigidh.**
— *Will they understand?*
— *Yes.*

— **Am bruidhinn e riutha?**
— **Cha bhruidhinn.**
— *Will he speak to them?*
— *No.*

— **Am falbh i?**
— **Chan fhalbh.**
— *Will she go?*
— *No.*

EXERCISE 1 - TRANSLATE

Translate the following short Gaelic sentences into English.

1. **Fònaidh i gu Mustafa a-nochd.**

   ✎ _____

   _____

2. **Am fosgail mi an uinneag?**

   ✎ _____

   _____

3. **Dannsaidh sinn aig a' chèilidh.**

   ✎ _____

   _____

4. **Chan ith Ahmed is Zara feòil.**

   ✎ _____

   _____

5. **An ruith sibh no an coisich sibh?**

   ✎ _____

   _____

6. **Cha shuidh sinn idir.**

   ✎ _____

   _____

EXERCISE 2 - FILL IN THE GAPS

Fill in the gaps in the following sentences with the correct forms of the future tense.

1. Òlaidh mi fìon dearg ach ✎_____
   mi fìon geal.

2. ✎_____ i thuca a-màireach ach
   cha sgrìobh i an-diugh.

3. — ✎_____ sibh goilf feasgar?
   — Cluichidh.

4. — ✎_____ sinn an-dràsta?
   — Cha phàigh.

5. — Cha ghlan mi an càr sa mhadainn ach
   — ✎_____ mi e feasgar.

6. — ✎_____ sinn sa bhaile aig uair?
   — Coinnichidh.

EXERCISE 3 - REARRANGE

Sort the words in these sentences into the correct order so that they make sense. Then translate each sentence into English.

1. iad | cha | leam | stad | leig

   ✎_____

   _____

   _____

2. an | dhut | mi | rathad | seallaidh

✎_____

_____

_____

3. thu | aig | fuirich | an | doras | am | rium

✎_____

_____

_____

4. sinn | loch | anns | snàmhaidh | an

✎_____

_____

_____

5. i | ùr | an | am-bliadhna | càr | ceannaich

✎_____

_____

_____

6. an | reic | sin | idir | dealbh | mi | cha

✎_____

_____

_____

* * *

Well done! When you're ready, you can find the answers on page 244.

46

DREUCHDAN
VOCABULARY CONSOLIDATION

This activity is all about practising and consolidating vocabulary. The list below contains 20 words or phrases on the topic of work. Take a couple of minutes to familiarise yourself with the vocabulary, then cover up the list with your hand or a piece of paper and try to complete the exercises on the next few pages without looking at it. **Gur math a thèid leat!**

* * *

dreuchd (f) - occupation, profession
sanas-obrach (m) - job advert
a' cur a-steach airson obair - applying for a job
agallamh (m) - interview
pàirt-ùine - part-time
làn-ùine - full-time
cùrsa-beatha (f/m) - career
a' fastadh luchd-obrach - employing staff

luchd-fastaidh (m, pl) - employers

ag obair bhon taigh - working from home

fòrladh (m) **màthaireil / athaireil** - maternity / paternity leave

a' fàgail dreuchd - resigning, leaving a job

a' gluasad gu obair eile - moving to another job

gun obair - out of work, unemployed

ag obair tron oidhche - working nights

ag obair air a ceann / cheann fhèin - (she is / he is) self-employed

tuarastal (m/f) - wage, salary

ceannard (m) - boss

còraichean-obrach (f, pl) - working conditions

a' leigeil dheth dreuchd* - retiring

*Note that **a' leigeil dheth dreuchd** is the generic form for "retiring", but it changes to **a dhreuchd** when used in the masculine form and **a dreuchd** when used in the feminine form.

EXERCISE 1 - TRANSLATE

Cover up the vocabulary list and write down the Gaelic translation of the words and phrases below.

1. part-time

    ✎_____

2. working from home

    ✎_____

3. employers

✎ _____

4. resigning, leaving a job

✎ _____

5. employing staff

✎ _____

EXERCISE 2 - MISSING LETTERS

Fill in the missing letters to make words from the list on the topic of work.

1. t u _ _ a s t a _
2. c ù _ _ a – b e _ _ _ a
3. g _ n o b _ _ r
4. l à _ – ù i _ _
5. c _ _ n n a _ d

EXERCISE 3 - PLACE IN SEQUENCE

Put the following stages of progression in a career into the most logical order.

a) a' gluasad gu obair eile
b) a' leigeil dheth dreuchd
c) a' dol gu agallamh
d) a' faicinn sanas-obrach
e) a' cur a-steach airson obair

1. ✎_____
2. ✎_____
3. ✎_____
4. ✎_____
5. ✎_____

EXERCISE 4 - FILL IN THE GAPS

Fill in each gap in the sentences below with the most appropriate word or phrase from the list. Feel free to refer back to the list to help you.

1. 'S e nurs a th' annam. Bidh mi ag obair
   ✎_____ gu math tric
   anns an ospadal.

2. B' àbhaist Sean a bhith ag obair aig companaidh ach
   tha e ✎_____ a-nis.

3. Tha tuarastal math aice san dreuchd ùir ach chan eil
   na ✎_____ cho math idir.

4. Tha dùil aig Marilyn ri leanabh agus bidh i dol air
   ✎_____ a dh'aithghearr.

5. Bidh Mìcheal trì fichead sa còig bliadhna a dh'aois
   an-ath-bhliadhna agus bidh e
   ✎_____ a dhreuchd an
   uair sin.

* * *

When you're ready, you can find the answers on page 246.

47

AN CLÒ MÒR
READING FOCUS

The text below is about a Scottish fabric called **An Clò Mòr** ("the Big Cloth" or "the Big Tweed"), which is produced in the Outer Hebrides and is better known as Harris Tweed. Read the text, using the vocabulary list as required, before having a go at the comprehension and language exercises that follow. **Gabh romhad!**

* * *

'S e obair a' Chlò Hearaich aon de na gnìomhachasan as motha anns na h-Eileanan an Iar. Tha na ficheadan de dhaoine an sàs sa ghnìomhachas mar bhreabadairean is mar luchd-obrach ann am muilnean. Tha a' mhòr chuid de na breabadairean ag obair pàirt-ùine air beairtean ann an seadaichean aig an dachaighean fhèin. Bidh iad a' faighinn snàth a tha air a dhath a-cheana bho na muilnean clò is bidh iad ga fhighe ri chèile le beairtean a tha air an obrachadh le an làmhan is an casan. 'S e obair sgileil, eagnaidh a th' innte a tha a' tarraing ùine. Nuair a bhios na breabadairean deiseil leis a' chlò, bidh e a' dol don mhuilinn airson a sgrùdadh is a chrìochnachadh. Tha an clò air cliù a chosnadh mar aodach buan is blàth agus tha e air fàs air leth fasanta. Tha e air a chleachdadh ann an iomadh dòigh an-diugh ann an seacaidean, deiseachan, còtaichean, adaichean is ann am bagaichean, sporain is mar chòmhdach air àirneis.

VOCABULARY

gnìomhachas (m) - industry
an sàs ann - engaged in
breabadair (m) - weaver
muileann (m/f) - mill
a' mhòr chuid - most, the majority
beairt (f) - loom
seada (f/m) - shed
snàth (m) - thread
air a dhath - dyed, coloured
a-cheana - already
a' fighe ri chèile - weaving, knitting together
sgileil - skilful
eagnaidh - intricate, exact
a' tarraing ùine - taking time
deiseil - ready, finished
sgrùd - inspect, examine
crìochnaich - finish, complete
cliù (m) - fame, reputation
aodach (m) - clothes
buan - lasting, enduring
fasanta - fashionable
deise (f) - suit

còmhdach (m) - covering
àirneis (f) - furniture

EXERCISE 1 - COMPREHENSION

Answer the following questions in English.

1. Where do the weavers work?

   ✎_____

   _____

2. What do the mills provide to the weavers?

   ✎_____

   _____

3. What are we told about the nature of the weavers' work?

   ✎_____

   _____

4. What happens to the tweed when the weavers finish their work on it?

   ✎_____

   _____

5. What reputation does the tweed have?

   ✎_____

   _____

EXERCISE 2 - FIND THE GAELIC

Find the Gaelic translation of each of the following phrases from the text. Note that they don't appear in the order given below.

1. with their hands and feet

   ✎ _____

2. very fashionable

   ✎ _____

3. in many ways

   ✎ _____

4. most of the weavers

   ✎ _____

5. scores of people

   ✎ _____

EXERCISE 3 - CATEGORISE

Have another look at some of the vocabulary from our list laid out below – this time without the English translations – and sort the words according to their function.

gnìomhachas | breabadair | sgileil
a' tarraing ùine | muileann | beairt | eagnaidh
seada | sgrùd | snàth | a' fighe ri chèile
deiseil | crìochnaich | cliù | aodach | buan
deise | fasanta | còmhdach | àirneis

NOUNS:

✐ _____   ✐ _____

✐ _____   ✐ _____

✐ _____   ✐ _____

✐ _____   ✐ _____

✐ _____   ✐ _____

✐ _____

VERBS AND VERBAL PHRASES:

✐ _____   ✐ _____

✐ _____   ✐ _____

ADJECTIVES:

✐ _____   ✐ _____

✐ _____   ✐ _____

✐ _____

* * *

Once you've finished, you can turn to page 247 to check your answers.

AINMEARAN GNÌOMHAIREACH 1
GRAMMAR FOCUS

This Grammar Focus activity is about a particular type of verbal noun. You may already know that there are three types of verbal noun in Gaelic. These are called progressive, intent and complement.

If you've already completed Activity 7 in this book, you'll have had some practice in forming verbal nouns. In this activity, we will be looking at the progressive type of verbal noun.

* * *

PROGRESSIVE VERBAL NOUN + NOUN

The progressive type of verbal nouns are the ones that are normally used with the verb **bi** ("to be"). Examples include **a' coimhead** ("watching"), **a' fuireach** ("staying / living") and **ag èirigh** ("getting up / rising").

Nouns that follow progressive verbal nouns are in the genitive or possessive case when the noun is used with the definite article ("the"). Let's look at some examples:

Bha Lorna a' leughadh na litreach.
Lorna was reading the letter. (literally "reading of the letter")

Am bi thu a' glasadh an dorais air an oidhche?
Do you lock the door at night? (literally "locking of the door")

If the noun is not accompanied by a definite article, the genitive case is not used. In the example below, pay attention to **litir** used here instead of **litreach**, as in the example above.

Bha mi a' sgrìobhadh litir.
I was writing a letter.

PROGRESSIVE VERBAL NOUN + POSSESSIVE PRONOUN

Now, let's think about sentences in which the object (the person or thing that is the recipient of the action of a verb) is a personal pronoun. An example in English would be "I hear him", where "him" is the personal pronoun and the direct object of the sentence.

In Gaelic, when the object of a sentence is a personal pronoun, the verbal noun is not followed by a pronoun as in English. For example, we *can't* say **tha mi a' cluinntinn e**, translating "I am hearing him" word for word. Instead, we combine the **ag** or **a'** of the verbal noun with the appropriate possessive pronoun as shown on the next page. "I hear him" would therefore be **tha mi ga chluinntinn.**

The possessive determiners in Gaelic (usually known as "possessive pronouns") are:

singular		plural	
mo *my*		**ar**	*our*
do *your*		**ur**	*your*
a *his, her, its*		**an / am**	*their*

These are combined with the **ag / a'** of the verbal noun as follows:

singular		plural	
gam *at my*		**gar**	*at our*
gad *at your*		**gur**	*at your*
ga *at his, at her, at its*		**gan / gam***	*at their*

These combinations precede the verbal noun with which they are associated.

*Note that **gam** is used instead of **gan** before verbal nouns beginning with **b, f, m** or **p**.

MORE EXAMPLES

Let's now see some more examples of how they are used in sentences:

A bheil thu gam thuigsinn?
Do you understand me? (literally "are you at my understanding?")

Chan eil mi ga chreidsinn.
I don't believe him / it. (literally "I am not at his / its believing")

Bidh mi gur faicinn an-ath-sheachdain.

I'll see you (plural / formal) next week. (literally "I'll be at your seeing next week")

Some final notes about the possessive pronouns combined with **ag / a'**. The singular pronouns (**gam, gad** and the masculine **ga**) cause lenition in the following word, while the feminine **ga** and the plural pronouns don't.

Secondly, when a feminine possessive pronoun ends in a vowel and the verbal noun begins with a vowel, an **h-** is inserted before the verbal noun. For example:

ga h-oideachadh
educating her

Thusa nis! Now have a go at the exercises to put all of this into practice.

EXERCISE 1 - CHOOSE THE CORRECT WORD

Complete the sentences below by circling the correct word from the options given in bold. Then, translate the sentences into English.

1. Bha mi a' leughadh **leabhar / leabhair** air an trèana.

   ✎_____

   _____

2. Chan eil mi **gad / gar** chluinntinn ceart.

✎ _____

_____

3. Am bi thu a' fosgladh **an uinneag / na h-uinneige**?

✎ _____

_____

4. Cha robh i **gam / gan** tuigsinn idir.

✎ _____

_____

5. Bidh sinn **gan / ga** faicinn a-màireach.

✎ _____

_____

EXERCISE 2 - REARRANGE

Sort the words in these sentences into the correct order so that they make sense. Then, translate them into English.

1. **thu | a-nis | gam | bheil | chluinntinn | a**

✎ _____

_____

2. robh | san | coimhead | an | sibh | ga | ospadal

✎ _____

_____

3. gam | i | san | bha | àrd-sgoil | theagasg

✎ _____

_____

4. eil | gad | mi | idir | chreidsinn | chan

✎ _____

_____

5. iad | aig | gar | stèisean | bidh | an | coinneachadh

✎ _____

_____

EXERCISE 3 - TRANSLATE

Translate the following sentences. You'll be translating from Gaelic into English for the first three, then from English into Gaelic for the final three.

1. **Bha iad gar cuideachadh.**

✎ _____

_____

2. **Cò a tha a' togail an taighe?**

   ✎ _____

   _____

3. **A bheil thu gam faicinn a-nis?**

   ✎ _____

   _____

4. They are buying a new car.

   ✎ _____

   _____

5. Are you going to meet them?

   ✎ _____

   _____

6. He is seeing her tonight.

   ✎ _____

   _____

* * *

When you're ready, you can turn to page 249 to check your answers.

49

SLÀINTE
VOCABULARY CONSOLIDATION

This activity is all about practising and consolidating vocabulary. This time, we're focusing on the topic of health. Take some time to read through the list below of words to do with health, then cover up the list with your hand or a piece of paper and try to complete the exercises that follow without referring back to it. **Feuch ort!**

* * *

dotair (m)* - doctor
nurs (f)* / **banaltram** (f) - nurse
ionad-slàinte (m) - health centre
ospadal (m) - hospital
Roinn Tubaist is Èiginn (f) - accident and emergency department, emergency room
a' faireachdainn tinn / bochd - feeling ill, sick
a' faireachdainn nas fheàrr - feeling better

cràdh (m) - pain

ceann (m) **goirt** - headache, sore head

a' gearan - complaining

a' casadaich - coughing

goirtich - hurt

gearradh (m) - cut

plàst (m) / **pleastar** (m) - plaster, Band-Aid

pile (f/m) - pill

ìocshlaint (f) / **cungaidh-leighis** (f) - medicine, cure

òrdugh-cungaidh (m) - medical prescription

deuchainn-fala (f) - blood test

X-ghath (m) - X-ray

cuir fios air ambaileans - send for an ambulance

*While the grammatical gender of the noun **dotair** is masculine and of **nurs** is feminine, both terms can be used to refer to a doctor or nurse of any gender. For example, both **'s e nurs a th' ann** ("he is a nurse") and **'s e nurs a th' innte** ("she is a nurse") are correct sentences.

EXERCISE 1 - TRANSLATE

Cover up the list above and give the Gaelic translation for each of the words and phrases below.

1. headache

✎_____

2. a cut

✎_____

3. complaining

✎_____

4. hurt

✎_____

5. a pill

✎_____

EXERCISE 2 - DEFINITIONS

Write the Gaelic word or phrase that corresponds to each of the following definitions.

1. what you will need if you fall and break a bone

    ✎_____

2. how you feel when you are on the mend

    ✎_____

3. what you may be doing if you have a cold

    ✎_____

4. what you need in order to get your prescribed medicine from a pharmacy

    ✎_____

5. where you might need to go if you are involved in an accident

✎_____

6. what you use to cover and protect a cut

✎_____

EXERCISE 3 - FILL IN THE GAPS

Fill in the gaps in the sentences with the most appropriate word or phrase from the vocabulary list above. You can refer back to the list to help you if you need to.

1. **Cha robh Marion gu math. Bha i a'**
   ✎_____ **bochd.**

2. **Bha e a'** ✎_____ **fad na h-oidhche agus chaidh e dhan**
   ✎_____ **sa mhadainn.**

3. **Chuir an nurs** ✎_____ **air an ambaileans agus chaidh mo thoirt dhan**
   ✎_____.

4. **Ghoirtich mi mo chas a' cluich ball-coise is bha mi ann an** ✎_____.

EXERCISE 4 - COMPLETE THE SENTENCE

Circle the correct option to complete each sentence so that it makes sense.

1. Gheàrr mi mo làmh agus chuir an nurs **plàst** / **pile** air.
2. Ghabh mi deoch uisge agus bha mi faireachdainn **nas bochda** / **nas fheàrr.**
3. Cha robh Gary a' tuigsinn carson a bha an **gearradh** / **deuchainn-fala.**
4. Bha an cnatan oirre agus bha i **a' gearan** / **a' casadaich.**
5. Gheibh thu **ìocshlaint** / **ionad-slàinte** bhon dotair.

* * *

Once you have completed all the exercises, you can check your answers on page 250.

50

AINMEARAN GNÌOMHAIREACH 2: A' DOL
GRAMMAR FOCUS

If you've already completed Activity 48 in this book, you'll now know all about progressive verbal nouns. In this Grammar Focus, we'll be looking at another type of verbal noun in Gaelic, which is used to express intentions. **Nach tòisich sinn!**

* * *

EXPRESSING INTENDED ACTIONS

This type of verbal noun is used to express an intended action and is followed by a verb of motion. They are particularly commonly used after the verb **a' dol** ("going").

The verbal noun expressing intent is lenited where possible and is preceded by the particle **a**. When the verbal noun begins with a vowel or **fh** followed by a vowel, the **a** becomes **a dh'**.

Here are some examples:

A bheil thu a' dol a choiseachd dhan bhaile?
Are you going to walk to town?

Tha i a' dol a thoirt taing dhaibh.
She is going to thank them. (literally "to give them thanks")

Tha sinn a' dol a dh'fhuireach ann am Barraigh airson seachdain.
We're going to stay in Barra for a week.

Chaidh iad a dh'èisteachd ris a' chòmhlan ùr.
They went to listen to the new group.

The verbs **fòn** ("phone") and **sgrìobh** ("write") can also be followed by the verbal noun of intent. For example:

Fònaidh mi a dh'fhaighneachd cuin a tha a' chuirm-chiùil a' tòiseachadh.
I'll phone to find out when the concert starts.

Sgrìobhaidh mi a dh'iarraidh fios.
I'll write to ask for information.

VERBAL NOUN OF INTENT + NOUN

When a noun is used after the verbal noun of intent, it goes into the genitive or possessive case if it is accompanied by the definite article ("the"). For example:

Tha iad a' dol a cheannach an tuathanais.
They are going to buy the farm.

Bha iad a' dol a thomhas an fhearainn.
They were going to measure the land.

VERBAL NOUN OF INTENT + POSSESSIVE PRONOUN

As we saw in Activity 48, the progressive verbal noun can join with the possessive pronouns to create special combined forms.

The same happens with verbal nouns of intent, which we can combine with the possessive pronouns **mo, do, a, ar, ur** and **an / am** to give the particles **gam, gad, ga, gar, gur** and **gan / gam.**

Let's look at some examples of these forms in sentences expressing intentions:

Tha sinn a' dol gan coinneachadh aig a' phort-adhair.
We're going to meet them at the airport.

A bheil sibh a' dol gam faicinn a' cluich Disathairne?
Are you going to watch them play on Saturday?

Thusa nis! Now have a go at the exercises to put all of this into practice.

EXERCISE 1 - FILL IN THE GAPS

Fill in the gaps in the sentences below with the correct Gaelic form of the English verb provided.

1. **A bheil sibh a' dol a** ✎_____
   dhachaigh? (*walk*)

2. **Tha iad a' dol a** ✎_____ **aig a'**
   chèilidh. (*sing*)

235

3. Chan eil e a' dol a ✎_____
   a-màireach. (*work*)

4. Bha e a' dol a ✎_____ riutha.
   (*speak*)

5. Tha sinn a' dol a ✎_____ anns
   an taigh-òsta. (*stay*)

EXERCISE 2 - TRANSLATE INTO ENGLISH

Translate the following sentences expressing intention into English.

1. Tha a' chòisir a' dol a sheinn aig a' Mhòd am-bliadhna.

   ✎_____

   _____

2. Am bi iad a' dol a chluich goilf Disathairne?

   ✎_____

   _____

3. A bheil sibh a' dol a pheantadh an taighe?

   ✎_____

   _____

4. Chan eil sinn a' dol a ràdh càil mu dheidhinn.

   ✎_____

   _____

5. **Tha mi a' dol a dhùnadh a' gheata.**

✎ _____

_____

EXERCISE 3 - TRANSLATE INTO GAELIC

This time, we're translating into Gaelic.

1. She is going to read the book.

✎ _____

_____

2. I'm going to open the door.

✎ _____

_____

3. They were going to walk in the park.

✎ _____

_____

4. He is going to meet them at the station.

✎ _____

_____

5. Mary is going to see her.

_____

_____

* * *

When you're ready, you can turn to page 252 to check your answers.

ANSWERS
15-MINUTE COFFEE BREAKS

41. CEAP BREATAINN
Reading Focus

1. The island is 110 miles long and about 75 miles wide.
2. You see Scottish place names throughout the island and you meet many people with Highland Scottish names.
3. Hundreds of people from the Highlands of Scotland moved to Canada in the 19th century and many settled in Cape Breton.
4. In 1850 there were almost 100,000 Gaelic speakers in Nova Scotia. Today there are around 2,000 who have Gaelic / speak Gaelic.
5. The Gaelic College in St Anne's teaches Gaelic and runs classes in fiddling, piping, waulking songs and step dancing, among other things.

EXERCISE 2 - WRITE THE NUMBERS

1. seachdad sa còig mìle / trì fichead sa còig mìle deug
2. ceud, trithead sa dhà mìle neach / sia fichead sa dhà dheug mìle neach
3. ceud mìle neach / còig fichead mìle neach
4. (a' bhliadhna) ochd ceud deug is leth-cheud
5. dà mhìle neach

EXERCISE 3 - FIND THE GAELIC

1. tìr-mòr Alba Nuaidh
2. coinnichidh tu ri daoine gu leòr
3. san naoidheamh linn deug
4. tha cuid dhiubh ag ionnsachadh Gàidhlig
5. dh'fhosgail bun-sgoil Ghàidhlig

42. AN TRÀTH CAITHTE
Grammar Focus

EXERCISE 1 - FILL IN THE GAPS

1. ghabh
2. lìon
3. dh'fhòn
4. cha do chluich
5. cha do dh'èist
6. an do phàigh?
7. an do sgrìobh?

EXERCISE 2 - COMPLETE THE SENTENCES

1. **Sheinn** Sheila aig a' chèilidh.
2. **Cha do thill** iad fhathast.
3. **An do dh'èirich** sibh tràth?
4. **Cha do leugh** mi an leabhar sin.
5. **Nigh** Calum na soithichean.
6. Cuin a **dh'fhàg** an trèan Glaschu?

EXERCISE 3 - REARRANGE

1. **Cha do dhùin iad an geata.**
   TRANSLATION: *They didn't shut the gate.*
2. **An do ghabh sibh biadh san taigh-òsta?**
   TRANSLATION: *Did you have (literally "take") some food in the hotel?*
3. **Shuidh sinn faisg air an uinneig.**
   TRANSLATION: *We sat near the window.*
4. **An do chuir thu siùcar anns a' chofaidh?**
   TRANSLATION: *Did you put sugar in the coffee?*
5. **Stad am poileas an càr dubh.**
   TRANSLATION: *The police stopped the black car.*
6. **Thuit i agus bhris i a cas.**
   TRANSLATION: *She fell and broke her leg.*

43. SIUBHAL
Vocabulary Consolidation

EXERCISE 1 - TRANSLATE

1. **dòighean siubhail**
2. **cead-siubhail**

3. **air chall**
4. **a' ruighinn**
5. **a' fuireach ann an taigh-òsta**

1. **a' fàgail** ("leaving, departing")
2. **aiseag** ("ferry")
3. **clàr-siubhail** ("itinerary")
4. **a' dol cuairt** ("taking a trip / tour")

1. **a' dol air làithean-saora** ("going on holiday")
   ionad luchd-turais ("tourist office")
2. **stèisean thrèanaichean** ("train station")
   a' gabhail taigh air mhàl ("renting a house")
   port-adhair ("airport")
   a' lorg àite-fuirich ("finding a place to stay")

1. Gheibh thu fiosrachadh mu cheanglaichean aig an ionad **luchd-turais.**

   TRANSLATION: *You will get information about connections at the tourist office.*

2. Tha **dòighean siubhail** eadar-dhealaichte eadar Inbhir Nis agus Glaschu.

   TRANSLATION: *There are different modes of transport between Inverness and Glasgow.*

3. Feumaidh tu **cead-siubhail** airson a dhol a-null thairis.

   TRANSLATION: *You need a passport for going abroad.*

4. Bu chòir dhut coimhead air an **làraich-lìn** airson fios mu thaigh-òsta.

   TRANSLATION: *You should look at the website for hotel information.*

5. Is toil leinn a bhith **a' dol cuairt** anns a' phàirc.

   TRANSLATION: *We like going for a walk in the park.*

44. UISGE-BEATHA
Reading Focus

EXERCISE 1 - COMPREHENSION

1. There is great demand for Scotch whisky in many countries.
2. **Uisge-beatha** is equivalent to *aqua vitae* ("water of life") in Latin and the word "whisky" is based on the Gaelic word for "water", **uisge**.
3. There are over 150 distilleries in Scotland.
4. Strathspey is the most famous whisky production area and the word "glen" features in the names of many of the whiskies in that area.
5. Islay whisky has a special peaty flavour.

EXERCISE 2 - MATCH THE PHRASES

GAELIC	ENGLISH
1. **a' ciallachadh an aon rud**	D. *meaning the same (thing)*
2. **rim faighinn**	E. *to be found*
3. **o chionn iomadh linn**	B. *for many centuries*
4. **tha fèill mhòr air**	A. *it's in great demand*
5. **a' nochdadh tric**	C. *appears often*

EXERCISE 3 - FIND THE WORDS

1. dùthaich | sgìre | eilean | gleann
2. sgìre, sgìrean | taigh-staile, taighean-staile | eilean, eileanan
3. a-nis | linn | an-diugh
4. iomadh | ceud gu leth | tric | deich | mòran
5. ùra

45. AN TRÀTH TEACHDAIL
Grammar Focus

EXERCISE 1 - TRANSLATE

1. She'll phone Mustafa tonight.
2. Shall I open the window?
3. We'll dance at the ceilidh.
4. Ahmed and Zara will not eat meat.
5. Will you run or will you walk?
6. We won't sit at all.

EXERCISE 2 - FILL IN THE GAPS

1. Òlaidh mi fìon dearg ach **chan òl** mi fìon geal.
   TRANSLATION: *I'll drink red wine but I won't drink white wine.*
2. **Sgrìobhaidh** i thuca a-màireach ach cha sgrìobh i an-diugh.
   TRANSLATION: *She'll write to them tomorrow but she won't write today.*

3. — **An cluich** sibh goilf feasgar?

   — Cluichidh.

   TRANSLATION:

   — *Will you (plural / formal) play golf this afternoon?*

   — *Yes / We will / I will.*

4. — **Am pàigh** sinn an-dràsta?

   — Cha phàigh.

   TRANSLATION:

   — *Will we pay now?*

   — *No, we won't.*

5. Cha ghlan mi an càr sa mhadainn ach **glanaidh** mi e feasgar.

   TRANSLATION: *I won't clean the car in the morning but I'll clean it in the afternoon.*

6. — **An coinnich** sinn sa bhaile aig uair?

   — Coinnichidh.

   TRANSLATION:

   — *Will we meet in town at one o'clock?*

   — *Yes, we will.*

EXERCISE 3 - REARRANGE

1. **Cha leig iad leam stad.**

   TRANSLATION: *They won't let me stop.*

2. **Seallaidh mi an rathad dhut.**

   TRANSLATION: *I'll show you the way / road.*

3. **Am fuirich thu rium aig an doras?**

   TRANSLATION: *Will you wait for me at the door?*

4. **Snàmhaidh sinn anns an loch.**

   TRANSLATION: *We'll swim in the loch.*

5. **An ceannaich i càr ùr am-bliadhna?**

   TRANSLATION: *Will she buy a new car this year?*

6. **Cha reic mi an dealbh sin idir.**

   TRANSLATION: *I won't sell that picture at all.*

46. DREUCHDAN
Vocabulary Consolidation

EXERCISE 1 - TRANSLATE

1. **pàirt-ùine**
2. **ag obair bhon taigh**
3. **luchd-fastaidh**
4. **a' fàgail dreuchd**
5. **a' fastadh luchd-obrach**

EXERCISE 2 - MISSING LETTERS

1. **tuarastal** ("wage, salary")
2. **cùrsa-beatha** ("career")
3. **gun obair** ("out of work, unemployed")
4. **làn-ùine** ("full-time")
5. **ceannard** ("boss")

EXERCISE 3 - PLACE IN SEQUENCE

1. d) **a' faicinn sanas-obrach** ("seeing a job advert")
2. e) **a' cur a-steach airson obair** ("applying for a job")
3. c) **a' dol gu agallamh** ("going for an interview")
4. a) **a' gluasad gu obair eile** ("moving to another job")
5. b) **a' leigeil dheth dreuchd** ("retiring")

EXERCISE 4 - FILL IN THE GAPS

1. 'S e nurs a th' annam. Bidh mi ag obair **tron oidhche** gu math tric anns an ospadal.

   TRANSLATION: *I'm a nurse. I quite often work nights in the hospital.*

2. B' àbhaist Sean a bhith ag obair aig companaidh ach tha e **ag obair air a cheann fhèin** a-nis.

   TRANSLATION: *Sean used to work at / for a company but now he's self-employed.*

3. Tha tuarastal math aice san dreuchd ùir ach chan eil na **còraichean-obrach** cho math idir.

   TRANSLATION: *She has a good salary in the new job but the working conditions are not so good at all.*

4. Tha dùil aig Marilyn ri leanabh agus bidh i dol air **fòrladh màthaireil** a dh'aithghearr.

   TRANSLATION: *Marilyn is expecting a baby and she'll be going on maternity leave soon.*

5. Bidh Mìcheal trì fichead sa còig bliadhna a dh'aois an-ath-bhliadhna agus bidh e **a' leigeil dheth** a dhreuchd an uair sin.

   TRANSLATION: *Michael will be sixty-five years old next year and he will be retiring then.*

47. AN CLÒ MÒR
Reading Focus

EXERCISE 1 - COMPREHENSION

1. Most weavers work in sheds at their homes.
2. The mills provide yarn that is already dyed.

3. It is skilful, intricate and time-consuming work.
4. The tweed goes to the mill for inspection and finishing.
5. It has a reputation for being long-lasting and warm.

EXERCISE 2 - FIND THE GAELIC

1. le an làmhan is an casan
2. air leth fasanta
3. ann an iomadh dòigh
4. a' mhòr chuid de na breabadairean
5. na ficheadan de dhaoine

EXERCISE 3 - CATEGORISE

NOUNS:

- gnìomhachas
- breabadair
- muileann
- beairt
- seada
- snàth
- cliù
- aodach
- deise
- còmhdach
- àirneis

VERBS AND VERBAL PHRASES:

- a' tarraing ùine
- sgrùd
- a' fighe ri chèile
- crìochnaich

ADJECTIVES:

- sgileil
- eagnaidh
- deiseil
- buan
- fasanta

48. AINMEARAN GNÌOMHAIREACH 1
Grammar Focus

EXERCISE 1 - CHOOSE THE CORRECT WORD

1. Bha mi a' leughadh **leabhar** air an trèana.
   TRANSLATION: *I was reading a book on the train.*
2. Chan eil mi **gad** chluinntinn ceart.
   TRANSLATION: *I'm not hearing you properly / I can't hear you properly.*
3. Am bi thu a' fosgladh **na h-uinneige**?
   TRANSLATION: *Will you open / be opening the window?*
4. Cha robh i **gan** tuigsinn idir.
   TRANSLATION: *She didn't understand them at all.*
5. Bidh sinn **ga** faicinn a-màireach.
   TRANSLATION: *We'll see / be seeing her tomorrow.*

EXERCISE 2 - REARRANGE

1. A bheil thu gam chluinntinn a-nis?
   TRANSLATION: *Can you hear me now? / Are you hearing me now?*
2. An robh sibh ga coimhead san ospadal?
   TRANSLATION: *Were you seeing her in hospital?*
3. Bha i gam theagasg san àrd-sgoil.
   TRANSLATION: *She taught me / was teaching me in high school.*
4. Chan eil mi gad chreidsinn idir.
   TRANSLATION: *I don't believe you at all.*
5. Bidh iad gar coinneachadh aig an stèisean.
   TRANSLATION: *They'll meet us / be meeting us at the station.*

EXERCISE 3 - TRANSLATE

1. They were helping us.
2. Who is building the house?
3. Can / Do you see them now? / Are you seeing them now?
4. **Tha iad a' ceannach càr ùr.**
5. **A bheil thu / sibh a' dol gan coinneachadh?**
6. **Tha e ga faicinn a-nochd.**

49. SLÀINTE
Vocabulary Consolidation

EXERCISE 1 - TRANSLATE

1. **ceann goirt**
2. **gearradh**
3. **a' gearan**
4. **goirtich**
5. **pile**

EXERCISE 2 - DEFINITIONS

1. **X-ghath** ("X-ray")
2. **a' faireachdainn nas fheàrr** ("feeling better")
3. **a' casadaich** ("coughing")
4. **òrdugh-cungaidh** ("medical prescription")
5. **Roinn Tubaist is Èiginn** ("A & E")
6. **pleastar / plàst** ("plaster, Band-Aid")

EXERCISE 3 - FILL IN THE GAPS

1. Cha robh Marion gu math. Bha i a' **faireachdainn** bochd.

   TRANSLATION: *Marion wasn't well. She was feeling ill.*

2. Bha e a' **casadaich** fad na h-oidhche agus chaidh e dhan **ionad-slàinte** sa mhadainn.

   TRANSLATION: *He was coughing all night and he went to the health centre in the morning.*

3. Chuir an nurs **fios** air an ambaileans agus chaidh mo thoirt dhan **Roinn Tubaist is Èiginn.**

   TRANSLATION: *The nurse sent for the ambulance and I was taken to A & E.*

4. Ghoirtich mi mo chas a' cluich ball-coise is bha mi ann an **cràdh.**

   TRANSLATION: *I hurt my leg playing football and I was in pain.*

EXERCISE 4 - COMPLETE THE SENTENCE

1. Gheàrr mi mo làmh agus chuir an nurs **plàst** air.

   TRANSLATION: *I cut my hand and the nurse put a plaster / Band-Aid on it.*

2. Ghabh mi deoch uisge agus bha mi faireachdainn **nas fheàrr.**

   TRANSLATION: *I had a drink of water and I was feeling better.*

3. Cha robh Gary a' tuigsinn carson a bha an **deuchainn-fala.**

   TRANSLATION: *Gary didn't understand why he needed a blood test / what the blood test was for.*

4. Bha an cnatan oirre agus bha i **a' casadaich**.

   TRANSLATION: *She had a cold and she was coughing.*

5. Gheibh thu **ìocshlaint** bhon dotair.

   TRANSLATION: *You'll get medicine from the doctor.*

50. AINMEARAN GNÌOMHAIREACH 2: A' DOL
Grammar Focus

EXERCISE 1 - FILL IN THE GAPS

1. A bheil sibh a' dol a **choiseachd** dhachaigh?

   TRANSLATION: *Are you (formal / plural) going to walk home?*

2. Tha iad a' dol a **sheinn** aig a' chèilidh.

   TRANSLATION: *They're going to sing at the ceilidh.*

3. Chan eil e a' dol a **dh'obair** a-màireach.

   TRANSLATION: *He's not going to work tomorrow.*

4. Bha e a' dol a **bhruidhinn** riutha.

   TRANSLATION: *He was going to speak to them.*

5. Tha sinn a' dol a **dh'fhuireach** anns an taigh-òsta.

   TRANSLATION: *We're going to stay in the hotel.*

EXERCISE 2 - TRANSLATE INTO ENGLISH

1. The choir is going to sing at the Mòd this year.
2. Are they going to play golf on Saturday?
3. Are you going to paint the house?
4. We're not going to say anything about it.
5. I'm going to shut the gate.

EXERCISE 3 - TRANSLATE INTO GAELIC

1. Tha i a' dol a leughadh an leabhair.
2. Tha mi a' dol a dh'fhosgladh an dorais.
3. Bha iad a' dol a choiseachd anns a' phàirc(e).
4. Tha e a' dol gan coinneachadh aig an stèisean.
5. Tha Màiri a' dol ga faicinn.

ACKNOWLEDGEMENTS

This book has very much been a team effort and I would like to take the opportunity to thank the people who have helped to put it together.

Firstly, **tapadh leibh**, Chloe West, Claire Lipscomb and the whole team at Teach Yourself. It's been a pleasure to work with you all and we'd like to thank you for your belief in the project and your enthusiasm for helping us bring Coffee Break to a new audience around the world.

Mòran taing gu Susanna Naismith for her assistance in the early stages of the development of *50 Gaelic Coffee Breaks* and for the key role she played in the creation of the Coffee Break Gaelic course.

Ceud mìle taing gu Boyd Robertson, who has brought his huge experience in Gaelic education to the writing of the activities in this book, helping you to practise and improve your Gaelic in a fun and effective way.

Taing mhòr gu Ava Dinwoodie, our Series Editor, whose dedication to the project and expert coordination meant that everyone knew exactly what they were doing and when it needed to be done!

Finally, thank you for reading the book and we very much hope you have enjoyed building your skills in Gaelic with us.

You may recall my mention of jazz virtuoso Charlie Parker in the Introduction to this book who, by focusing on practice, practice, practice, was then ready to fly and enjoy his performance. I hope that you're now feeling ready to let go and incorporate the new vocabulary, expressions and grammatical structures into your Gaelic on a daily basis.

Mark Pentleton – Founder, Coffee Break Languages

SHARE YOUR THOUGHTS

If you'd like to help other learners like yourself discover Coffee Break Gaelic, we'd be very grateful if you would consider leaving an honest review. If you bought the book online, you can do this easily by going to the website where you found it.

Tapadh leat! Thank you for sharing your thoughts and for helping other learners practise their Gaelic on their Coffee Break.

NOTES

NOTES

NOTES

RAISING READERS
Books Build Bright Futures

Dear Reader,

We'd love your attention for one more page to tell you about the crisis in children's reading, and what we can all do.

Studies have shown that reading for fun is the **single biggest predictor of a child's future life chances** – more than family circumstance, parents' educational background or income. It improves academic results, mental health, wealth, communication skills, ambition and happiness.[1]

The number of children reading for fun is in rapid decline. Young people have a lot of competition for their time. In 2024, 1 in 10 children and young people in the UK aged 5 to 18 did not own a single book at home.[2]

Hachette works extensively with schools, libraries and literacy charities, but here are some ways we can all raise more readers:

- Reading to children for just 10 minutes a day makes a difference
- Don't give up if children aren't regular readers – there will be books for them!
- Visit bookshops and libraries to get recommendations
- Encourage them to listen to audiobooks
- Support school libraries
- Give books as gifts

There's a lot more information about how to encourage children to read on our website: **www.RaisingReaders.co.uk**

Thank you for reading.

hachette
UK

---

[1] OECD, '21st-Century Readers: Developing Literacy Skills in a Digital World', 2021, https://www.oecd.org/en/publications/21st-century-readers_a83d84cb-en.html

[2] National Literacy Trust, 'Book Ownership in 2024', November 2024, https://literacytrust.org.uk/research-services/research-reports/book-ownership-in-2024

ALSO BY COFFEE BREAK LANGUAGES

Are you also learning another language? Or do you have a friend or relative who's a learner of a different language? Our *50 Coffee Breaks* series also includes books in English, French, Italian, German, Swedish, Mandarin Chinese and Spanish, available both in paperback and as ebooks.

Just visit fiftycoffeebreaks.com.

See you soon, à bientôt, a presto, bis bald, vi ses, 再见 zàijiàn and ¡hasta pronto!

MORE COFFEE BREAK LEARNING

Here at Coffee Break Languages we provide learning through podcasts, courses, videos and books. For more learning from Coffee Break, just visit:

coffeebreaklanguages.com/gaelic

Find us on your favourite social media platform by searching for Coffee Break Languages.

Chì sinn a dh'aithghearr thu!

facebook.com/coffeebreaklanguages

x.com/coffeebreaklang

instagram.com/coffeebreaklanguages

youtube.com/@coffeebreaklanguages